Psalms Of Discipleship:

A One Year Journey With The Shepherd

(Volume 1)

Psalm 1:1 ~ Psalm 27:9

52 Weekly Bible Studies & Devotions

SOMETHING *new*

Psalms of Discipleship: A One Year Journey With The Shepherd

(Volume 1)

Psalm 1:1 ~ Psalm 27:9

Psalms of Discipleship is written as a tool for the people of God to use in order to grow in their faith and then to pass it on to other believers. The

DR. DENNY BATES
LEADING WITH QUALITY IN MIND

Dedication

To all of the members of the Facebook group, Psalms of Discipleship.

I will always be grateful for your willingness to walk with me on this Journey with the Shepherd of the Psalms

The things which you have heard from me in the presence of many witnesses, entrust these to faithful men who will be able to teach others also. 2 Timothy 2:2

Table of Contents

Psalms of Discipleship Devotions: Quarter Number Two (13 Weeks)

Psalms of Discipleship Devotions: Quarter Number Four (13 Weeks)

Deeper Study Tools:

Foreword: An Introduction to the Disciped Life

A spiritual legacy should be the goal of every believer who has placed his or her trust in the saving grace of Jesus Christ. This should be the goal, but far too many have set their sights on a mediocre and diluted version of living the Christian life. Instead of experiencing a healthy pace of spiritual growth over the course of a lifetime, there is a stagnation, a dullness, a lethargic attempt to know Christ and grow closer to Him. The apostle Paul shared with us his passion and utmost desire for his life when he said,

> But whatever things were gain to me, those things I have counted as loss for the sake of Christ. More than that, I count all things to be loss in view of the surpassing value of knowing Christ Jesus my Lord, for whom I have suffered the loss of all things, and count them but rubbish so that I may gain Christ, and may be found in Him, not having a righteousness of my own derived from *the* Law, but that which is through faith in Christ, the righteousness which *comes* from God on the basis of faith, that I may know Him and the power of His resurrection and the fellowship of His sufferings, being conformed to His death; in order that I may attain to the resurrection from the dead. (Phil 3:7-11)

No doubt, spiritual growth is a challenge for every believer, no matter the life experiences or culture in which he or she lives. Spiritual growth does not come easy; many times it is just plain hard. But just because it is hard, does not excuse us from the need to experience spiritual growth. In order to grow spiritually, it takes effort: effort that is supernaturally undergirded by the grace of God. It takes obedience and a clear decision to follow the Lord. Pastor and writer Rick Warren underscores this when he writes, "Spiritual growth is not automatic. It takes an intentional commitment. You must *want* to grow, *decide* to grow, *make an effort* to grow, and *persist* in growing. Discipleship—the process of becoming like Christ—always begins with a decision. Jesus calls us, and we respond: "'Come, be my disciple,' Jesus said to him. So Matthew got up and followed him'" (Warren 2002, *The Purpose-Driven Life*. p. 179).

The call for believers to live a discipled life of spiritual growth is timeless and essential. The world is waiting for a reason to follow the claims of Jesus Christ, looking to those who are experiencing an authentic faith that is appealing, growing and redeeming. The Church is waiting for men and women to live out what they know to be true as disciples of Jesus Christ, allowing the Church to be the Church as it impacts the world in which we live. The disciple of Jesus Christ is waiting for a strategy, for a plan, for a movement that he or she can join to lead others to a more vibrant relationship with Jesus Christ. It is my hope to clearly lay out the case for the eternal value in making a commitment to living the discipled life. It is a commitment to quality relationships as underscored by Paul's words to the Thessalonian believers when he said, "Having thus a fond affection for you, we were well-pleased to impart to you not only the gospel of God but also our own lives, because you had become very dear to us" (1 Thess. 2:8).

There is a legacy being made by every believer who follows Jesus Christ. The question that should motivate each one is this: what kind of a disciple have I been? "The challenge to count the cost of discipleship means the difference between posing as a disciple and living as one" (Wilkins 1992, *Following the Master: Discipleship in the Steps of Jesus.* p. 357).

It is my hope that Psalms of Discipleship will become a useful tool for you, the reader, to learn how to better live as a disciple of Jesus Christ. The format is simple, by design. The commitment to apply the Psalms to your life is up to you. May we all begin to experience a fresh approach to spiritual growth by living the discipled life with the help of grace, worship, Bible study, prayer, community, service, and evangelism.

Growing in grace with you,

Denny Bates | Florence SC | December, 2011

How to Use This Book

Would You Like To Take A Fresh Look At God's Word?

Over the years as I have studied, observed, and personally experienced spiritual growth, I have come to the right conclusion that one of the key catalysts to a believer's spiritual growth is not just Bible study for the sake of information, but the kind of Bible study that leads the believer to reflect upon what is being read. Some call it a "quiet time." Others call it "personal devotions." Call it what you will, but I call it an "essential spiritual practice" if one desires authentic and measurable spiritual growth.

Each week you are invited to spend some time reading and reflecting upon "Psalms of Discipleship," a simple, easy to use devotional experience. By spending five minutes or fifty-five minutes on the weekly devotion, you will be afforded the opportunity to enhance your spiritual growth.

Psalms of Discipleship: *How does it work?*

Part 1: The Scripture and the Core Value

Each week in your devotional book you will discover <u>a key scripture</u> from a Psalm, written out for you. Read the passage and reflect upon it, asking God to speak to your heart. He so desires to talk to you. Please give Him time, and listen.

Then, there is <u>a specific core value of discipleship</u> (a means of growth) associated with this scripture. As we take this spiritual journey through the Psalms, we will discover together the seven core values that mark the life of the one who is following Jesus as His disciple. They are grace, worship, Bible study, prayer, community, service, and evangelism. Each week, we will all be challenged with this question: is this core value woven into the fabric of my life?

Part 2: Simple Commentary of Explanation

In a paragraph or two, the core principle is discussed in practical ways that make sense and provoke deeper thought for further study.

Part 3: The Principle, the Application, the Time to Reflect and Respond, the Prayer of Response

The Biblical Principle is based upon the passage from Psalms that the disciple of Jesus Christ seeks to adapt to his or her life.

The Application is simple and straightforward. This will help you unpack the meaning of this passage and how it applies to your life. Don't rush through it, but carefully, prayerfully, think through each point.

Reflect & Respond: Some Really Good Questions To Ponder is for when you may wish to find some quality time in your day to think through these thought-provoking questions. As with the application, do not rush through these questions, but give yourself time to dialogue with God on what you are thinking.

The Prayer offered at the end helps you summarize your thoughts. You may use this prayer as a beginning point. Feel free to add to it.

The Balanced Triad Of Biblical Discipleship: *How does it work?*

A brief note of explanation: As you study this chart (see page 16), seek to view each part of the chart as related to every other part. It all begins with a RELATIONSHIP (with God and with others), which leads to DOCTRINE (what we believe in and are challenged to do), which then leads to PERSONAL APPLICATION (putting into action what we know to do). For the quality disciple, this leads us up through the triangle of grace, worship, Bible study, prayer, community, service, and then evangelism. This is a never-ending journey of discipleship and spiritual growth. In other words,

> For the quality disciple, it all begins with having a foundation of **grace** . . . where we can then **worship** God in the way He prefers . . . then, and only then, will we be able to experience genuine **spiritual growth (Bible study, prayer, community)** . . . where we will then be able to **serve** as we share our spiritual gifts . . . and as we experience God's grace, worship Him as He sees fit, grow in our relationship with Him, and serve using our gifts for Him, we will then have an authentic **witness** to the lost using both our words and our deeds. (Mission Statement **D**isciple**M**akers**4J**esus—DM4J)

It is my strong conviction that a person who is discipled will be given every opportunity to succeed and become a quality disciple—one who is maturing in the characteristics specific to living as a biblical disciple of Jesus Christ. The discipled believer will be capable and confident to make disciples as one is willing to deepen one's own relationship with Him.

One final word: This spiritual growth resource is designed with the intent to assist in the reader's spiritual maturity. I hope and pray that your time in the Scriptures will be a personal blessing to you. But even more, I pray that you will take your experience and invest in the lives of others. In other words,

The things which you have heard from me in the presence of many witnesses, entrust these to faithful men who will be able to teach others also. 2 Timothy 2:2

As you experience this devotional book (read it, pray through it, share it), begin to think forward and invite a friend to join you and offer to disciple them. Your life and their life will never be the same again!

Are you ready to begin this journey? Remember: a quality *disciple* makes a quality *life*. May the Lord allow us to all live as quality disciples of His.

THE BALANCED TRIAD OF BIBLICAL DISCIPLESHIP

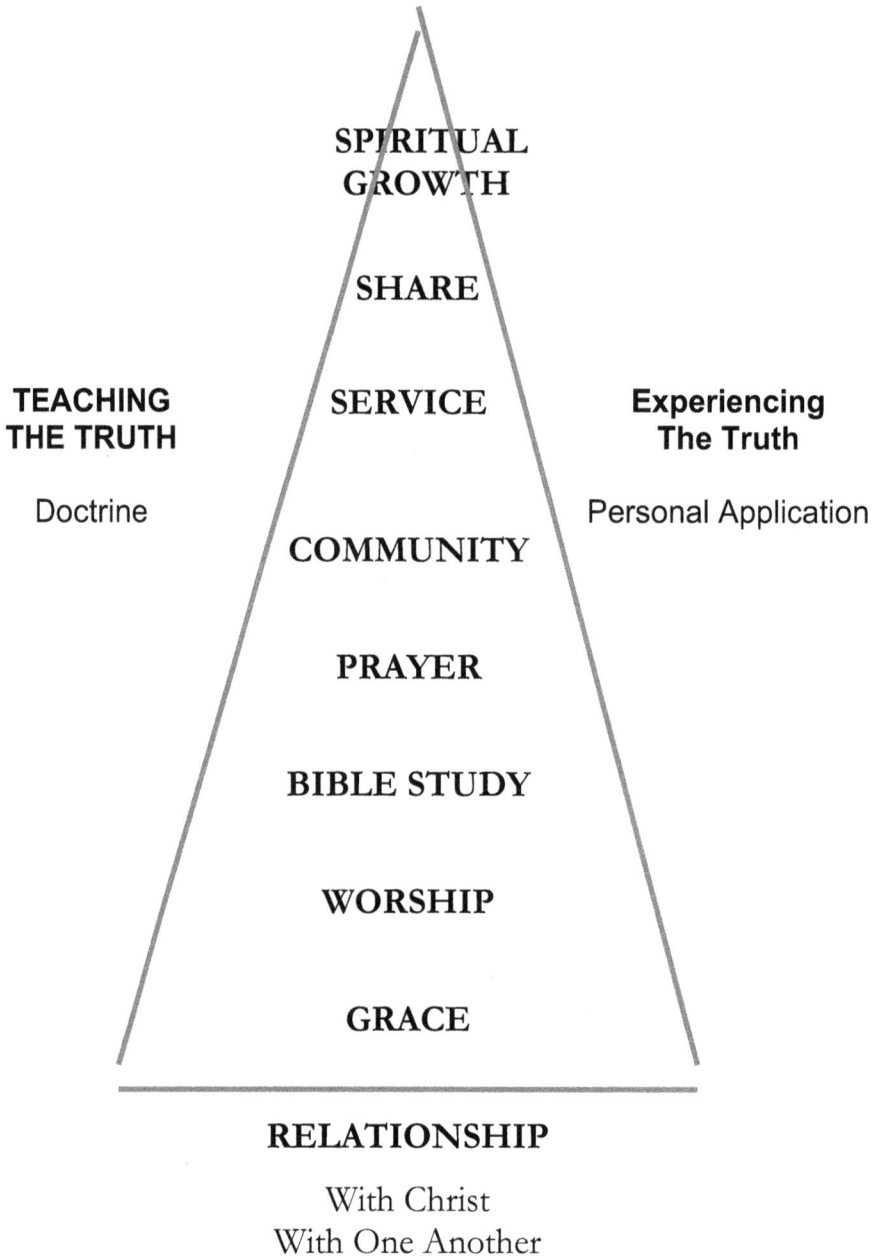

SPIRITUAL
GROWTH

SHARE

TEACHING   SERVICE   **Experiencing**
THE TRUTH   **The Truth**

Doctrine   Personal Application

COMMUNITY

PRAYER

BIBLE STUDY

WORSHIP

GRACE

RELATIONSHIP

With Christ
With One Another

Psalms of Discipleship—Principle #1

Life Principles For Those Who Choose To Follow Jesus And Live The Discipled Life

Key Scripture: How blessed is the man who does not walk in the counsel of the wicked, Nor stand in the path of sinners, Nor sit in the seat of scoffers **Psalm 1:1**

Core Value: Community

Connecting in community is not an option if one wishes to grow in faith and in relationship. The answer for a meaningful relationship and spiritual growth is not isolation nor a program steeped in religious rituals. What really matters in Christian spiritual formation is the relationship with other believers. "Ironically, one problem we often see in the Christian community is that people get more into religion and less into the connectedness the Bible prescribes, with the result that they get sicker" (How People Grow: Cloud & Townsend 2001, 123). It was the great writer and thinker John Donne who stated these timeless words: "No man is an island unto himself." This simply means that it is crucial for a believer who wishes to grow spiritually to have frequent times of fellowship with other like-minded believers. In addition to times of corporate worship, time must be spent in a smaller group setting in order to build lasting, meaningful relationships. There is a great need for a healthy community of believers who are committed to building authentic relationships.

Principle #1 & Personal Application: Quality disciples place great value in being a part of a biblical community with other disciples of Christ.

The quality disciple:

- Refuses to walk in the counsel of the wicked; instead, seeking out those who are godly and wise.
- Refuses to stand in the path of sinners; instead, surrounding themselves with those who are seeking a right relationship with Jesus Christ.
- Refuses to sit in the seat of scoffers; instead, keeping themselves from those who poison the heart with doubt and unbelief and seeking out those who believe God.

Reflect & Respond: Some Really Good Questions To Ponder...

Who are the people I trust the most with my life?

In what ways am I blessed with the company I keep?

Prayer:

Lord Jesus, thank You for allowing me to be a member of the body of Christ. Continue to guide me into the kind of relationships with other disciples that will strengthen my relationship with You.

". . . we need spiritual friends, *broken* people who will provide safety for us to be broken, *caring* people who want us to live and believe we can live well, *giving* people who pour the life they have received from God into us, people of *vision* who see the Spirit shaping us into the image of Christ. Without them, we settle for so much less." Pg. 41; Crabb, Larry. 1999. *The safest place on earth: where people connect and are forever changed.* Nashville, TN: Word Publishing.

Psalms of Discipleship—Principle #2

Life Principles For Those Who Choose To Follow Jesus And Live The Discipled Life

Key Scripture: [2] But his delight is in the law of the LORD, And in His law he meditates day and night. [3] He will be like a tree *firmly* planted by streams of water, Which yields its fruit in its season And its leaf does not wither; And in whatever he does, he prospers. **Psalm 1:2-3**

Core Value: Bible Study

Every believer needs to spend quality time in God's Word. Systematic study, expository study, devotional study, thematic study should be a part of every believer's Christian experience. If a believer is committed to reading and studying his or her Bible every day, spiritual growth will come. But it is important to note: the goal of Bible study is not just about collecting "Bible trivia." Bible study or Bible "reading" must lead to change, not just to be adorned with more intellectual information.

Principle #2 & Personal Application: Quality disciples place great value in spending quality time in God's Word.

- Bible study should never be a drudgery, an activity done out of a legalistic obligation. Spending time in God's Word should be a delight!
- Bible study is not limited to a one-time event but has a residual effect upon the entire day—meditating on it both night and day.
- The fruit of having an ongoing experience with the Bible is spiritual growth and a prosperous life.

Reflect & Respond: Some Really Good Questions To Ponder...

Does the time I spend in the Word of God give me delight?

Is it my habit to read my Bible for information's sake or to reflect upon what I read and see how I can apply it to my life?

What one thing can I do today that will enrich my reading of the Bible?

Prayer:

Lord Jesus, may I always have a hunger, a longing for Your Word. May I not only look at Bible study as a necessary spiritual discipline but also see it as a way to grow in my relationship with You, becoming closer to You.

Psalms of Discipleship—Principle #3

Life Principles For Those Who Choose To Follow Jesus And Live The Discipled Life

Key Scripture: Worship the LORD with reverence And rejoice with trembling. **Psalm 2:11 (NASB95)**

Serve the LORD with fear and rejoice with trembling. **Psalm 2:11 (NIV)**

Core Value: Worship & Service

God is worthy of our worship and service because He is God and He has made everything. The human heart that has been filled with the presence of Christ has no other choice but to worship and serve the One who made everything. He and He alone is worthy of our worship and service. Worship of and service to God is such a privilege. The quality disciple is moved by the fact that the same God who made heaven, earth, the sea, and the springs of water, made him or her too. Just think; the One who created EVERYTHING large and small, took the time not to just create mankind. He also took the time to send a REDEEMER who would save us from our sins. Such a God should have our unending worship and service! God has no interest in us giving Him half-hearted worship and service. For the person who has yet to experience unhindered worship of and service to God, he or she will never gain God's best for them. True worship and service is much more than a ritual—it is a relationship with the Lord God Almighty.

Principle #3 & Personal Application: Quality disciples choose a way of life that is driven by a passionate worship of God expressing itself in humble service to Him.

- The disciple of Jesus Christ does not compartmentalize his or her worship and service to God. Instead, worship and service is all consuming.
- We must worship and serve God as He desires—to do so with a holy reverence and acute awareness of who He is (Almighty God)…and who we are (sinners, saved by grace).
- It is humility that helps us to better appreciate and live out the discipled life, as one who desires to follow Jesus Christ.

Reflect & Respond: Some Really Good Questions To Ponder...

How do I really know that I am worshiping God in a way that pleases Him?

Is my life being defined as personal selfishness or by sacrificial service?

Prayer:

Lord Jesus, what a mighty and awesome God You are! May my worship never be watered down to a religious habit. Instead, may my relationship with You be grounded in my worship and service to You.

The Essential Core Values Of The Quality Disciple Are...
Grace—Worship—Bible Study—Prayer—Community—Service—Evangelism

Psalms of Discipleship—Principle #4

Life Principles For Those Who Choose To Follow Jesus And Live The Discipled Life

Key Scripture: But You, O LORD, are a shield about me, My glory, and the One who lifts my head. **Psalm 3:3**

Core Value: Grace

Grace is the foundational core value of a disciple's life. When the Christian life is viewed through the prism of God's grace, God is viewed in a brand new way.

> People do not grow until they shift from a natural human view of God to a real, biblical view of God. *The first aspect of that shift has to be the shift from a God of law to the God of grace. People must discover that God is for them and not against them.* This is what it means to have a God of grace . . . One of the biggest obstacles to growth is our view of God. If we are going to grow in relation to God, then we must know who God is and what he is really like (How People Grow by Cloud & Townsend 2001, 66).

For the Christian who is experiencing the grace of God and learning how to integrate it on a consistent basis, there is a renewed sense of relief and feelings of safety. God is for them and not a threat to them. Grace is the essential core value that helps the disciple appreciate the gravity of how desperately needy we are of the Savior. Fortunately for us, God knows. God knows that we need the kind of grace that makes us completely dependent upon Him.

Principle #4 & Personal Application: Quality disciples deeply acknowledge and appreciate the gracious care of the Lord. He is the One who shields us and who gently lifts our head in order for us to see His face.

- The disciple of Jesus Christ knows Him as the LORD. He is God and has sovereign power over His people.
- It is the LORD who shields us, covers us, cares for us; He protects us from our enemies.

- When we are down and discouraged it is the Lord Jesus who gently lifts our countenance so that we might better see His face.

Reflect & Respond: Some Really Good Questions To Ponder...

How do I relate to Jesus as LORD? Is there anything that I have failed to yield control over to Him?

Is there anything going on in my life (a heaviness of my heart) that needs lifting by the Lord?

Prayer:

Lord Jesus, You know me well. You are God and I am not. Forgive me when I want to wrest away from You control of my life. Thank You for being my Lord, my God, my shield, my glory, and the One who lifts my head.

"The late pastor and Bible scholar Donald Barnhouse perhaps said it best: 'Love that goes upward is worship; love that goes outward is affection; love that stoops is grace.'" Pg. 7; Swindoll, Charles, R. 2003. *The Grace Awakening.* Nashville, TN: W Publishing Group.

Psalms of Discipleship—Principle #5

Life Principles For Those Who Choose To Follow Jesus And Live The Discipled Life

Key Scripture: I was crying to the LORD with my voice, And He answered me from His holy mountain. Selah. **Psalm 3:4**

Core Value: Prayer

It is through prayer that we have the opportunity to breathe in heaven's air. Prayer is a time of communion. It is meant to be a dialogue, not simply a monologue. Prayer is the power for the believer's life that enhances spiritual growth. Prayer, simply put, is having a conversation with God. Prayer is a time to listen to the Lord's small, still voice; it is a passionate articulation of what is on our mind; it is the most intimate time of sharing the concerns of our life; and it is the deep cry of the human heart directed toward God. Prayer then, is a dialogue, not a monologue where only one voice is heard. "To the LORD I cry aloud, and he answers me from his holy hill. Selah" (Psalm 3:4 NIV) and further illustrated by the psalmist: "Out of the depths I cry to you, O LORD; O Lord, hear my voice. Let your ears be attentive to my cry for mercy" (Psalm 130:1-2 NIV). Prayer is not a sterile communication system. Instead, prayer with God is all about cultivating an ongoing love relationship.

Principle #5 & Personal Application: Quality disciples experience an intimate and interactive dialogue with God in prayer.

- The person who follows Jesus Christ knows the One who wants to hear the cry of our heart.
- Because there is a personal relationship between Jesus and the disciple, prayer is more than just a futile exercise. Instead, prayer becomes the very language of intimacy.
- Prayer is not a monologue. Prayer is a dialogue. How wonderful it is when the disciple pauses to listen and hear from God. Selah (chew on this—ponder it, think about it, meditate on it).

Reflect & Respond: Some Really Good Questions To Ponder...

Can I sense any difference in the intensity of my prayer, not only when I pray to God in my *mind*, but also use my *voice* to speak out loud to Him?

What do I need to improve upon in my life in order to better listen to God when He speaks to me?

Prayer:

Lord Jesus, it is such a blessing to me that You not only want me to talk to You about my life, but You also want to talk to me about Your life. May our conversations always help me become more like You.

The Essential Core Values Of The Quality Disciple Are...
Grace—Worship—Bible Study—Prayer—Community—Service—Evangelism

Psalms of Discipleship—Principle #6

Life Principles For Those Who Choose To Follow Jesus And Live The Discipled Life

Key Scripture: Answer me when I call, O God of my righteousness! You have relieved me in my distress; Be gracious to me and hear my prayer. **Psalm 4:1**

Core Value: Prayer

      Andrew Murray suggests that the prayer life of the believer is not about getting things from God, but a much more meaningful and relational experience than the Lord serving as some kind of cosmic bellhop for us. "Prayer is not merely coming to God to ask something of Him. It is, above all, fellowship with God and being brought under the power of His holiness and love, until He takes possession of us and stamps our entire nature with the lowliness of Christ, which is the secret of true worship" (Living A Prayerful Life, 1983, pg. 46). One's prayer life must be more than just a vain ritual that has no meaning to it. Prayer, biblical prayer, must be deeply personal.

Principle #6 & Personal Application: Quality disciples fully expect God to answer prayer.

- This kind of dynamic prayer life is not founded upon a variety of man-made methods (works), but is founded upon having a vibrant relationship with the Lord Jesus (grace).
- It is because of the righteousness of Jesus Christ that the disciple can have a relationship with the One who does answer prayer.
- When the burdens of this world seek to crush us, Jesus Christ is the One who relieves us in our distress. Sometimes, He even chooses to remove that which is causing us distress. Always, He is with us in our distress.

Reflect & Respond: Some Really Good Questions To Ponder…

When I pray *why* do I expect God to answer me?

What kind of distress (physical, mental, emotional, spiritual) am I facing this week? In what ways has the Lord been at work in me during this time?

Prayer:

Lord Jesus, please remind me to come to You—first—when I am undergoing times of distress. Forgive me for the times when I seek to rescue myself using my own strength and wit. Grant me the faith to trust You with my life. May I truly believe that You will be gracious to me and hear my prayer.

"What the church needs today is not more machinery or better, not new organizations or more and novel methods, but men whom the Holy Spirit can use—men of prayer, men mighty in prayer. The Holy Spirit does not flow through methods, but through men. He does not come on machinery, but on men. He does not anoint plans, but men—men of prayer." Pg. 447; Bounds, E. M. 2004. *The complete works of E. M. Bounds on prayer.* Grand Rapids, MI: Baker Books.

Psalms of Discipleship—Principle #7

Life Principles For Those Who Choose To Follow Jesus And Live The Discipled Life

Key Scripture: But know that the LORD has set apart the godly man [and woman] for Himself; The LORD hears when I call to Him. **Psalm 4:3**

Core Value: Grace & Prayer

It is the grace of God that allows the believer to grow deeper in relationship with the Lord. We can seek to improve our prayer life; to study the Bible on a regular basis; and to even fast and deny ourselves pleasure. But without the grace of God, all of it is for naught. Grace is given to the believer not just for one's personal gratification. Grace is also a gift to the community of believers. Grace for the believer is to be shared by the believer to the believer. Grace is to be modeled. We all are to be trophies of His grace. The great challenge for every disciple is to become so marinated with the grace of God that we live a transformed life. It is a life we cannot "will" to do in our own strength, but a life where we lay down our will and live for His.

Principle #7 & Personal Application: Quality disciples personally experience God's grace. Quality disciples are blessed because they are personally experiencing God's grace *and* authentic prayer. Because of grace, we (the disciple of Jesus) can pray to the Lord who hears us. Disciples of Jesus Christ can become a disciple because of what God has done through the finished work of Christ. Through grace, we have been placed "in Christ." Through grace, we can communicate with the Lord through prayer.

- Because of His Word to us, His sure promise to us, we can *know* that the Lord has set apart the godly man (and woman) for Himself. Disciples of Jesus Christ belong to Him!
- Because disciples of Jesus Christ belong to Him, we have been given access to Him through prayer.
- "The Lord hears." What an amazing promise: to think that the sovereign God and Lord of the universe, the King of Glory, would not only hear the cry of our heart, but also loves and cares for us.

Reflect & Respond: Some Really Good Questions To Ponder...

What kind of lifestyle is the Lord calling me to live since He has set apart the godly man (and woman) for Himself?

When is the last time that I have cried out to the Lord?

Prayer:

      Lord Jesus, I am in awe of You. Thank You for loving me, for setting me apart, for choosing me to be one of Your children. As a disciple of Jesus Christ, teach me to pray; please help me to develop a more intimate, more authentic relationship with You.

The Essential Core Values Of The Quality Disciple Are...
Grace—Worship—Bible Study—Prayer—Community—Service—Evangelism

Psalms of Discipleship—Principle #8

Life Principles For Those Who Choose To Follow Jesus And Live The Discipled Life

Key Scripture: [1] Give ear to my words, O LORD, Consider my groaning. [2] Heed the sound of my cry for help, my King and my God, For to You I pray. [3] In the morning, O LORD, You will hear my voice; In the morning I will order *my prayer* to You and *eagerly* watch. **Psalm 5:1-3**

Core Value: Prayer

Prayer is what Henri Nouwen suggests to be, "a great adventure." This great passion that lies in the heart of the quality disciple to pray is best learned . . . by praying. In Christian bookstores today are a multitude of books dedicated to the subject of prayer. There is no lack of materials concerning the subject of prayer. But in spite of all the "how to" books, none of those books will pray for the disciple. From the heart of each believer must come the willingness to go beyond the theory behind prayer and to begin praying. Sometimes one needs to just take "baby steps" when one wants to renew one's commitment to pray. Small successes go a long way with the person who wants to develop a deeper prayer life. A quality disciple will become a man or woman of prayer.

Principle #8 & Personal Application: Quality disciples have dynamic lives, marked by the spiritual discipline of prayer and a firm expectation that God is at work.

- A life of prayer goes beyond the superficial. Instead, the disciple offers to the Lord a prayer that uses words (both spoken and unspoken), passionate groaning, as he or she cries for help.
- A life of prayer is God-centered and not me-centered. The disciple directs his or her prayer to the Lord, to "my King and my God. For to You I pray."
- A life of prayer is driven by spiritual discipline: "In the morning I will order my prayer to You." The disciple is willing to make a sacrifice of time.
- A life of prayer is given the privilege of having a front row seat as we "eagerly watch" how God is going to work through our prayers to Him.

Reflect & Respond: Some Really Good Questions To Ponder...

When I pray, what is my expectation of the Lord? Is the foundation of my prayer life God-centered or me-centered?

What one thing can I do this week that will enhance my prayer life?

Prayer:

Lord Jesus, You offer great comfort to those who pray to You—knowing that You not only hear the deepest concerns of my heart but You also are working for Your glory and for my good. May my prayer life to You become mature as I learn to trust You more.

"The Word of God is the fulcrum upon which the lever of prayer is placed, and by which things are mightily moved. God has committed himself, his purpose, and his promise to prayer. His Word becomes the basis, the inspiration of our praying, and there are circumstances under which, by importunate prayer, we may obtain an addition, or an enlargement of his promises . . . There would seem to be in prayer the capacity for going even beyond the Word, of getting even beyond his promise, into the very presence of God, himself. Jacob wrestled, not so much with a promise, as with the promise. We must take hold of the promiser, lest the promise prove inoperative." Pg. 67; Bounds, E. M. 2004. *The complete works of E. M. Bounds on prayer.* Grand Rapids, MI: Baker Books.

Psalms of Discipleship—Principle #9

Life Principles For Those Who Choose To Follow Jesus And Live The Discipled Life

Key Scripture: But as for me, by Your abundant lovingkindness I will enter Your house, At Your holy temple I will bow in reverence for You. **Psalm 5:7**

Core Value: Worship

"Few individuals deny the importance of worship, but relatively few understand what it means or have a passion to engage God through worship" (George Barna). What does it really mean to "worship" God? The general meaning of the word "worship" is pregnant with meaning. To worship means that we are to bow down, to give reverence to, to adore, to pay homage to. In the New Testament, the English word worship comes from the Greek word, proskuneo. It is where we get the English word, "prostrate." In the Old Testament, there are two primary meanings of the word worship. One meaning implies a devoted servant. The other meaning suggests a bowing down to. Combined, the Old Testament concept is more than a ritual or an academic exercise—it is a vibrant story of God coming down and telling His people how He wanted to be approached; how He wanted to be worshiped. William Temple illustrates what it means to worship God when he said, "To worship is to quicken the conscience by the holiness of God, to feed the mind with the truth of God, to purge the imagination by the beauty of God, to open the heart to the love of God, to devote the will to the purpose of God."

Principle #9 & Personal Application: Quality disciples have a keen and reverent respect for the Lord and hearts that seek to worship God.

A heart that seeks to worship God:

- Is aware of the Lord's abundant lovingkindness.
- Will do so in a holy temple. (The disciple is His Temple; see 1 Corinthians 6:19, 20)
- Will be Christ-centered and not man-centered.
- Will bow down and be reverent to Him.

33

Reflect & Respond: Some Really Good Questions To Ponder...

When I seek to worship the Lord am I often distracted by other people around me, beside me, in front of me?

What can I do to make my worship of God not a hollow and ritualistic obligation, but an authentic and meaningful way of life?

Is my heart in the right condition; where it is a holy temple, a place where a proper worship of God can take place?

Prayer:

Lord Jesus, I so desire that my worship of You count for something more than just an emotional feeling and superficial high that flames out when the moment fades. I want to know You more, to love You more, to worship You more; and to worship You in the way it pleases You.

The Essential Core Values Of The Quality Disciple Are...
Grace—Worship—Bible Study—Prayer—Community—Service—Evangelism

Psalms of Discipleship—Principle #10

Life Principles For Those Who Choose To Follow Jesus And Live The Discipled Life

Key Scripture: [11] But let all who take refuge in You be glad, Let them ever sing for joy; And may You shelter them, That those who love Your name may exult in You. [12] For it is You who blesses the righteous man, O LORD, You surround him with favor as with a shield. **Psalm 5:11-12**

Core Value: Grace and Worship

Grace and worship are forever coupled together. Because of grace, we can worship God in a way that pleases Him. Because of worship, we gain an even deeper appreciation for His grace. When the believer learns how to worship God and then do so in love and obedience, spiritual growth will occur. James MacDonald says it well. One needs to have the right view of God when he writes, "A. W. Tozer rightly observed that what you think about God is the most important thing about you. It's true whether you realize it or not: your entire life revolves around your view of God" (Downpour. 2006, pg. 49).

Principle #10 & Personal Application: Quality disciples, deeply moved by the grace of God, experience unbridled joy that results in adoration and praise.

- It is God's grace that causes a disciple to worship because a safe refuge can be found in the Lord. We are *glad*.
- It is God's grace that causes a disciple to worship because the song of joy has no end. We are *filled*.
- It is God's grace that causes a disciple to worship because they personally experience the blessings promised to the righteous man and woman. We are *blessed*.

Reflect & Respond: Some Really Good Questions To Ponder...

When I feel threatened and ill at ease, how do I find my refuge in the Lord?

When I am depressed, what promises does God provide me according to this Psalm?

Prayer:

Lord Jesus, there are certainly times during my spiritual journey where I feel a bit wayward and detached from You. Thank You for the reminder from Your Word that You have promised me a refuge, a personal gladness, a song of joy, and the blessing that comes according to the impartation of Your righteousness in my life. You do surround me with favor as with a shield.

"A. W. Tozer rightly observed that what you think about God is the most important thing about you. It's true whether you realize it or not: your entire life revolves around your view of God." Pg. 49; MacDonald, James. 2006. *Downpour.* Nashville, TN: Broadman & Holdman.

Psalms of Discipleship—Principle #11

Life Principles For Those Who Choose To Follow Jesus And Live The Discipled Life

Key Scripture: The LORD has heard my supplication, The LORD receives my prayer. **Psalm 6:9**

Core Value: Prayer

Who is to pray? Every believer is to pray. No one is exempt from the joy and responsibility of having a dialogue with God. God, the Creator and Sustainer of the Universe, has requested the presence of His children (Heb. 4:15-16). It is through prayer that the believer can approach the throne of grace and receive mercy and find grace to help us in one's time of need. A quality disciple understands the unique privilege that God has given. The benefit of the discipline of prayer is that it will help the disciple grow spiritually. A disciple who is trained to pray will become a mover and shaker in one's generation.

Principle #11 & Personal Application: Quality disciples not only *pray* to the Lord, but also know that God *hears*.

- The Lord not only hears our prayer, but receives it, accepts it, captures it and treasures this intimate conversation with the Creator God and His creation.
- The Lord has an ear to hear even the whispered cries for help from the deepest and darkest parts of our soul.
- The Lord takes delight in having a conversation with His disciples.

Reflect & Respond: Some Really Good Questions To Ponder...

When I pray, how confident am I in my heart that He is interested in listening to me?

What kinds of prayer requests are heavy on my heart today?

Prayer:
> *Lord Jesus, what an amazing thing it is that You not only hear my prayer (imperfect as it may be), but You receive my prayer; You do not ignore me and turn me away. Please remind me to trust You with the concerns of my heart, both great and small; for You, O Lord, intimately care for me.*

The Essential Core Values Of The Quality Disciple Are...
Grace—Worship—Bible Study—Prayer—Community—Service—Evangelism

Psalms of Discipleship—Principle #12

Life Principles For Those Who Choose To Follow Jesus And Live The Discipled Life

Key Scripture: O LORD my God, in You I have taken refuge; Save me from all those who pursue me, and deliver me, **Psalm 7:1**

Core Value: Prayer

When are we to pray? The Bible says that God's people are to pray without ceasing, to pray always—night and day (1 Thess. 3:10; 1 Tim. 5:5; Acts 10:2; 1 Thess. 5:17). One of the biggest challenges to hurdle in the area of developing a dynamic prayer life is to understand that prayer is just like breathing; without it one may die spiritually. There is the great need to pray night and day, to pray regularly, to pray continually. It takes an effort to pray. The quality disciple is more than willing to invest one's time in something that will produce eternal results. It all boils down to a choice of the will—will the disciple pray? And, are we praying enough? Richard Foster makes an excellent point about the frequency of prayer in the believer's life. He believes that Christians tend to pray more than one thinks: "Countless people, you see, pray far more than they know. Often they have such a 'stained-glass' image of prayer that they fail to recognize what they are experiencing as prayer and so condemn themselves for not praying." Self-condemnation = spiritual defeat. Grace richly applied in prayer = spiritual victory!

Principle #12 & Personal Application: Quality disciples know that prayer offered in Jesus' name will lead them to put trust in the One who is their Refuge.

- When we are surrounded by our enemies, we need to remember our relationship with "O LORD my God."
- When our circumstances are bleak and all hope seems lost, we need to remember where we take refuge; in the name of the LORD our God.
- When we take refuge in the LORD we find ourselves in a place of great strength, protection, and safety. This is the wonderful promise of Scripture: *The name of the LORD is a strong tower; The righteous runs into it and is safe.* **Proverbs 18:10 (NASB95)**

Reflect & Respond: Some Really Good Questions To Ponder...

When I sense spiritual danger, how do I find my way into the safe place the Lord provides?

What will make my prayer life effective when there is a war of challenging circumstances raging around me?

Prayer:

Lord Jesus, You are my Refuge, my Protector, my Shield, my Defender, my Deliverer, and my Guard. May it be said of me that when my enemies seek to drive me away from what I know to be true, I would take refuge and put my trust in the One who is the lover of my soul.

"Love is the syntax of prayer. To be effective pray-ers, we need to be effective lovers...Real prayer comes not from gritting our teeth but from falling in love." Pg. 3; Foster, Richard. 1992. P*rayer: finding the heart's true home.* San Francisco, CA: HarperSanFrancisco.

Psalms of Discipleship—Principle #13

Life Principles For Those Who Choose To Follow Jesus And Live The Discipled Life

Key Scripture: I will give thanks to the LORD according to His righteousness And will sing praise to the name of the LORD Most High. **Psalm 7:17**

Core Value: Worship

Giving thanks and singing praise is an act of worship to God. But it must be done so with a whole heart. As the Scripture clearly states, the disciple is to "Love God with all of your heart, Love God with all your soul, Love God with all your mind, Love God with all your strength" (Mk.12:30). According to this verse in the Gospel, one can make at least three observations: The big ideas in this passage are…

- It is a personal love—"You shall love the Lord your God."

- It is a committed love—"You shall love the Lord your God will ALL" you have got.
- It is a consummate love—"You shall love the Lord your God with all your HEART . . . your SOUL . . . your MIND . . . your STRENGTH."

This kind of love is based upon a sacrifice: "How can you tell if you love the Lord Jesus Christ? It hinges on whether you are willing to make the ultimate sacrifice for His will as a daily thing" (John MacArthur). This kind of love and worship is single minded and focused upon obedience.

Principle #13 & Personal Application: Quality disciples practice a worship that is centered upon the character and majesty of God.

- Worship of Jesus must be based upon who God is (the God of the Bible), not what we want Him to be (the God of our own expectation).
- Worship of Jesus is a worship that evokes a vibrant thanksgiving to the Lord.

- Worship of Jesus is filled with songs of praise to His name, to the Lord Most High.

Reflect & Respond: Some Really Good Questions To Ponder...

When I worship the Lord, is my mind focused upon His character and greatness or is it upon what I want Him to do for me?

How can the use of my Bible enhance my worship of God?

Prayer:

Lord Jesus, You are so beautiful to me. For me, You are my Wonderful Counselor, my Mighty God, my Everlasting Father, and my Prince of Peace. You are Faithful and True, Mighty to Save, the Alpha and Omega, the Bright and Morning Star, the Lily of the Valley, the Fairest of Ten Thousand, the Good Shepherd, the Great I AM, the Author and Finisher of my Faith, the Bread of Life, the Chief Cornerstone, the Rock, the Messiah, the Vine, the Great High Priest, the King of kings and Lord of Lords, the King of Glory, the Lamb of God, the Light of the World, the Resurrection and the Life, the Living Word of God. You are all this...and so much more. You are my Lord.

"The central issue of values is summed up in what Jesus called the first and greatest commandment: 'Love the Lord your God with all your heart and with all your soul and with all your mind' (Matthew 22:37). This is the value to value. This is the prism through which all other values must shine, the filter through which all of life's choices are made and solutions are drawn. Until we have learned to love God properly, the rest of what we have learned about values will remain an academic exercise." Pg. 49-50; Boa, Kenneth. *The perfect leader: practicing the leadership traits of God.* Colorado Springs, CO: Victor (Cook Communications Ministries).

Psalms of Discipleship—Principle #14

Life Principles For Those Who Choose To Follow Jesus And Live The Discipled Life

Key Scripture: O LORD, our Lord, How majestic is Your name in all the earth, Who have displayed Your splendor above the heavens! **Psalm 8:1**

Core Value: Worship

Worship that focuses upon the Lord will lead us to an even greater depth of love. That we can even love God, others, or even ourselves is because He took the initiative first (this is called "grace") and loved us (Rom. 5:8; 1 Jn. 4:19-21). The point of discipleship is not the creation of another church program that occupies the time of already busy believers. The point of discipleship is not even about doing all of the spiritual exercises well and knowing all of the Bible trivia answers. Discipleship is all about love.

This "Great Command" to love and worship God (Mark 12:30) is the very foundation of the Christian life, and consequently, living out the discipled life as the Bible teaches. Everything we do is measured by the way we love God, the way we love our neighbors, the way we love our self. In other words, the command to love God completely and to love our neighbor as we love our self is an expectation for everyone who claims the name of Christ. Biblical discipleship is an all or nothing proposition. Far too many have watered down the kind of love commitment Jesus wants His followers to embrace.

Principle #14 & Personal Application: Quality disciples are overwhelmed with awe and wonder of who God is.

- There is a worship that is *personal*: the Lord is my Lord
- There is a worship that is *corporate*: the Lord is our Lord
- There is a worship that *celebrates* the majesty of His name: there is no name like His name
- There is a worship that helps me *focus* upon the greatness and magnificence of God: there is no one like my great and mighty Lord

43

Reflect & Respond: Some Really Good Questions To Ponder...

What do I need to do in order to expand my view of God's greatness and majesty?

Every disciple has a distinctive worship *personality*. What is my pathway or "style" of worship? Do I best respond in my worship of Jesus Christ when (1) I commune with God in nature; (2) I am alone in solitude, reading, reflecting, praying; (3) I am in a "worship" service with many other believers; (4) I am surrounded by a wide array of appealing sights, smells, and sounds that stimulate; (5) I am with a small group of other disciples of Christ; (6) I am serving others by using the gifts God has given me? (This thought inspired by Gary Thomas in "Sacred Pathways"; Zondervan)

Prayer:
Lord Jesus, there is no one like You. You are the Lord, my Lord, our Lord. Your name is majestic. When I say Your name out loud, worship for You rises up in my soul. Your greatness is everywhere on the earth and in the heavens above. May I never lose my sense of awe and wonder for who You are.

The Essential Core Values Of The Quality Disciple Are...
Grace—Worship—Bible Study—Prayer—Community—Service—Evangelism

Psalms of Discipleship—Principle #15

Life Principles For Those Who Choose To Follow Jesus And Live The Discipled Life

Key Scripture: [4] What is man that You take thought of him, And the son of man that You care for him? [5] Yet You have made him a little lower than God, And You crown him with glory and majesty! [6] You make him to rule over the works of Your hands; You have put all things under his feet, **Psalm 8:4-6**

Core Value: Service

Many have wondered why God did not take them immediately into heaven upon the point of their conversion. Why did He delay their departure? It is because He has a plan for their life here on planet earth. It is a plan that was set in place before they were even born. It is a plan of service, of doing good works (Eph. 2:10). God has prepared the disciple to be His servant. All one needs is a little bit of encouragement from the Scriptures in order to learn what God has gifted one to do; and then to get involved in what He has already prepared the believer to do—to serve. What a phenomenal thought: God had a plan of service for the Christian's life before they were born. What a comfort, what a joy, to serve within the structure of His will for His people.

The pressure is off! God's people do not need to worry what to do for the Lord. He has gifted them, equipped them, and prepared them to do His will. The quality disciple comes to have this great assurance of God's sovereignty in their life—God has prepared each believer to serve Him. Brad Waggoner reminds us that service is not an option to the disciple of Jesus Christ. "Since we are created to produce good works, serving others simply isn't an option (pg.110). . . . Every Christian is created to produce good works. Service to God and others is not an a` la carte offering on a spiritual menu; it's part of the main course" (pg. 111). Waggoner, Brad J. 2008. *The shape of faith to come: spiritual formation and the future of discipleship.* Nashville, TN: B&H Publishing Group.

Principle #15 & Personal Application: Quality disciples are responsible and devoted managers of God's assets.

- It is a great honor to be created and cared for by the Creator God of the universe
- It is a great honor to be given the privilege to be crowned with glory and majesty
- It is a great honor to be tasked with the job of managing His assets

Reflect & Respond: Some Really Good Questions To Ponder...

What is the most important task that God has given me to manage for Him?

How is my service to God impacting those who are closest to me?

Prayer:

Lord Jesus, what a blessing it is to know that I am in Your thoughts and that You really care for me. What an honor it is that You would desire to crown me with glory and majesty. What a responsibility You have given to me: to rule over the works of Your hands. May I always be found faithful as I serve You.

"Our best contribution in life—our 'utmost for his highest'—can only be made as we allow God to finish his work in progress and perfect our uniqueness. To live without discovering our uniqueness is to not really live." Pg. 21; Rees, Erik. 2006. *S.H.A.P.E.: finding and fulfilling your unique purpose for life.* Grand Rapids, MI: Zondervan.

Psalms of Discipleship—Principle #16

Life Principles For Those Who Choose To Follow Jesus And Live The Discipled Life

Key Scripture: [1] I will give thanks to the LORD with all my heart; I will tell of all Your wonders. [2] I will be glad and exult in You; I will sing praise to Your name, O Most High. **Psalm 9:1-2**

Core Value: Worship

Is it reasonable to say that one's worship of God can be directly linked to one's spiritual growth? For instance, if one's worship is shallow and superficial there will be little spiritual growth because there will be no intimacy; there will be no relationship; there will be no transformational growth. In contrast, if one's worship is deep and authentic there will be measurable spiritual growth because it is real; it is personal; it is intentional: "I will" worship God with a passionate heart that sets out to know Him.

Spiritual growth is not considered an option for those who desire to have a biblical relationship with the Lord Jesus. Spiritual growth is a must. It is the life of discipleship that shepherds the desiring soul into a closer walk with Him. The Scriptures clearly teach that everyone is needy for the Lord, desperately so. Every believer is in need of the discipled life, because without it, we can fool ourselves into thinking that we are something that we are not—spiritually sufficient. We need to worship God with a passion or else we will simply fade away into a life of meaningless religious activities. Worship is the marvelous tool that God uses to give Him great glory and to give us great good.

Principle #16 & Personal Application: Quality disciples practice an active and vibrant worship of God.

As I worship God:

- *I will* give thanks to the Lord with all my heart
- *I will* tell of all His wonders
- *I will* be glad and exult in Him
- *I will* sing praise to His name

47

Reflect & Respond: Some Really Good Questions To Ponder...

How would my view of my life's circumstances be different if I began to give thanks to the Lord with <u>all my heart</u>?

What do I have to cultivate in my life that will make my worship of God active and vibrant?

Prayer:

       Lord Jesus, may I worship You: not with a half-hearted effort, but with a whole and devoted heart. May I tell of all of Your wonders: to tell others what I have seen You do in my own life. May I be glad and exult in You: to make the choice to give You the glory and honor and praise You so deserve from me. And Lord, May I sing praise to Your name: I will let no rock or any other created thing out-praise me (Luke 19:40; Psalm 69:34).

The Essential Core Values Of The Quality Disciple Are...
Grace—Worship—Bible Study—Prayer—Community—Service—Evangelism

Psalms of Discipleship—Principle #17

Life Principles For Those Who Choose To Follow Jesus And Live The Discipled Life

Key Scripture: [9] The LORD also will be a stronghold for the oppressed, A stronghold in times of trouble; [10] And those who know Your name will put their trust in You, For You, O LORD, have not forsaken those who seek You. **Psalm 9:9-10**

Core Value: Grace

A Grace-Driven life is the key to a deeper relationship with the Lord. The success of discipleship is when the experience becomes personal, sort of an "ah ha" moment, when it all begins to make sense. One goes far beyond the actual mechanics of discipleship into a deeper relationship with Jesus Christ. Dallas Willard says this well as he writes, "As a disciple of Jesus I am with him, by choice and by grace, learning from him how to live in the kingdom of God . . . I am not necessarily learning to do everything he did, but I am learning how to do everything I do in the manner that he did all that he did . . . For a disciple of Jesus is not necessarily one devoted to doing specifically religious things as that is usually understood. To repeat, I am learning from Jesus how to lead my life, my whole life, my real life" (The Divine Conspiracy, 283).

I agree with Willard. Discipleship is all about relationship and a genuine love for Jesus Christ. It is a humble desire to learn about Him and to know and then practice His ways. A disciple of Jesus Christ seeks to give away one's life, their whole life, away to Him and His care. When a person's love for Jesus grows, then discipleship is well on the way to being described as a success.

Principle #17 & Personal Application: Quality disciples have the confident assurance that there is a safe place in Him.

- The grace of God provides a stronghold: a place of protection for the oppressed believer, for the believer who is experiencing times of trouble
- The grace of God allows the believer to know the name of God
- The grace of God allows the believer to put their trust in Him

- The grace of God allows the believer to have the kind of authentic relationship with a faithful Lord who does not forsake those who seek Him

Reflect & Respond: Some Really Good Questions To Ponder...

When I feel oppressed by my circumstances, what has been my typical response? Do I place my trust in myself, in others, or in the Lord?

As I think about my relationship with the Lord, why is it important for me to know His name?

Prayer:

Lord Jesus, what a marvelous provision of grace You have given to me. How blessed I am to have a Lord who provides a stronghold, a place of safety and comfort, when I am oppressed and feeling troubled. How blessed I am to have a Lord who has revealed Himself to me and invites me to place my trust in Him. How blessed I am to know that You will never forsake me. How blessed...I...am.

"What seems so right is, in fact, heresy—the one I consider the most dangerous heresy on earth. What is it? *The emphasis on what we do for God, instead of what God does for us.*" Pg.15; Swindoll, Charles, R. 2003. *The Grace Awakening*. Nashville, TN: W Publishing Group.

Psalms of Discipleship—Principle #18

Life Principles For Those Who Choose To Follow Jesus And Live The Discipled Life

Key Scripture: O LORD, You have heard the desire of the humble; You will strengthen their heart, You will incline Your ear **Psalm 10:17**

Core Value: Prayer

Where are we to pray? From the Scriptures shown below, the believer is given at least four examples of where they are to pray. One is to pray in secret (Mt. 6:5-6). One is to pray at home (Acts 12:12). One is to pray in public, for example in a church (Acts 3:1). One is to pray with a small group of other believers (Mt. 18:19-20). The Christian life is portable, meaning that we are not bound to express our faith in only "religious" places. A disciple's prayer life can be taken beyond the church building and into the streets—wherever one goes—where prayer can do the most good. Training a disciple to feel comfortable praying anywhere God leads them is a key part of spiritual growth. How does one do this? It is done by living it out before others with one's own life and example. It is imperative that leaders set the tone when it comes to prayer. This is especially true as it pertains to discipleship.

> "When it comes to prayer, leaders set the tone. What is important to them becomes important to the people. Prayer begins in the leader's private prayer closet. Then it moves out to the people of God. Spiritual leaders must teach about prayer, model prayer, and lead others to pray. There is no right way to do this; there are many right ways. Leaders must choose a strategy and follow it." (The Shape of Faith To Come. Waggoner 2008, 223)

Principle #18 & Personal Application: Quality disciples know the Lord—are intimately acquainted with Jesus—and are known by Him.

When we live a prayerful life:

- Our deepest desires are intimately expressed to the Lord
- Humility is formed in our character, helping us to live out what we believe
- Our hearts are strengthened to persevere when everything around seeks to overwhelm and defeat us

51

- We have the ear, the focused attention, of the Lord of the Universe who intently listens to the heart cry of His people

Reflect & Respond: Some Really Good Questions To Ponder...

What kinds of practical things can I do that will enhance my knowledge of the Lord?

When my heart is weak and my faith is down, how does my prayer time with the Lord encourage me?

Prayer:

Lord Jesus, thank You that You hear the heart and desire of the humble. I am grateful that through prayer You will strengthen my heart. I am so thankful that You have both the time and the personal interest in me to listen to the concerns of my heart. Teach me, help me, encourage me, to enrich my prayer life. I do want to know You better than I do. I want the kind of Christian experience where prayer is not just another thing to do, but a way of life.

The Essential Core Values Of The Quality Disciple Are...
Grace—Worship—Bible Study—Prayer—Community—Service—Evangelism

Psalms of Discipleship—Principle #19

Life Principles For Those Who Choose To Follow Jesus And Live The Discipled Life

Key Scripture: For the LORD is righteous, He loves righteousness; The upright will behold His face. **Psalm 11:7**

Core Value: Worship

Do we have a proper understanding of what it really means to worship God? Is our worship based upon our feelings and surrounding ambiance or is it much deeper than what is on the surface? There are far too many professing Christians who struggle with what it means to worship God. In his book "Growing True Disciples" George Barna says,

> "For most people, worship implies attending a church service that includes music and preaching. An underlying issue that must ultimately be resolved is that widespread ignorance among born-again adults regarding the meaning of worship. When we asked people to describe the meaning of worship, 42 percent of all adult believers were unable to provide a substantive or reasonable reply. Among the believers who gave a substantive answer, many gave answers like 'attending church' or listening to the sermon.' In total, 58 percent gave us a reasonable response. . . . Few individuals deny the importance of worship, but relatively few understand what it means or have a passion to engage God through worship." Pg. 59

I believe the Scriptures teach us that worship is a sacrifice and all about God and His glory.

Therefore I urge you, brethren, by the mercies of God, to present your bodies a living and holy sacrifice, acceptable to God, *which is* your spiritual service of worship. **Romans 12:1 (NASB95)**

Principle #19 & Personal Application: Quality disciples have a high and exalted view of Almighty God.

- Biblical worship has its focus upon the *character* of God—He is righteous

- Biblical worship has its focus upon the *pleasure* of God—He loves righteousness
- Biblical worship has its focus upon the *face* of God—He desires worship that is personal and intentional

Reflect & Respond: Some Really Good Questions To Ponder...

In what way does the righteousness of God impact how I live my life?

According to the teaching of Scripture, what makes me "upright" in the Lord's eyes?

What does it look like when I behold His face? What am I seeing and experiencing?

Prayer:
   Lord Jesus, You are the Righteous One! There is no One like You. Your very nature is one of righteousness. You love it; You demonstrate it; You challenge me to love it too. The longer I gaze at Your face, the more I become like You. May I live in such a way that my character is impacted by Your righteousness, that I would come to love Your righteousness, and that I would seek Your face continually as I worship You.

Psalms of Discipleship—Principle #20

Life Principles For Those Who Choose To Follow Jesus And Live The Discipled Life

Key Scripture: The words of the LORD are pure words; As silver tried in a furnace on the earth, refined seven times. **Psalm 12:6**

Core Value: Bible Study

It is essential to understand why a proper understanding and practical application of grace and worship is critical when it comes to the core value of Bible study. Without grace and worship, Bible study becomes nothing more than a religious duty rather than a relational joy. Scot McKnight undergirds this need for a relationship when he writes in The Blue Parakeet, "If we are invited to love God by reading the Bible as God's communication with us, then a relational approach to the Bible invites us *to listen to God (the person) speak in the Bible and engage God as we listen* (pg. 89). . . . A relational approach believes *our relationship to the Bible is transformed into a relationship with the God who speaks to us in and through the Bible*" (pg. 90).

Principle #20 & Personal Application: Quality disciples have a high regard for the Word of God.

- The Bible, all of it, is trustworthy and true. There are no mistakes or errors. It is perfect in all its parts.

The law of the LORD is perfect, restoring the soul; The testimony of the LORD is sure, making wise the simple. **Psalms 19:7 (NASB95)**

- The Bible, all of it, has been given as God's Word to us. It is God's way of helping us grow in our faith.

[16] All Scripture is inspired by God and profitable for teaching, for reproof, for correction, for training in righteousness; [17] so that the man of God may be adequate, equipped for every good work. **2 Timothy 3:16-17 (NASB95)**

- The Bible, all of it, has stood the test of time and is eternal. All other books will come and go, but God's Word stands forever.

The grass withers, the flower fades, But the word of our God stands forever. **Isaiah 40:8 (NASB95)**

Reflect & Respond: Some Really Good Questions To Ponder...

How do I know for sure that my Bible translation is trustworthy and true?

Why is it important for me to give God's Word primacy in every area of my life: at home, at work, in my neighborhood, in my world?

Prayer:
> *Lord Jesus, may I never take Your Word for granted. Men and women have sacrificed so much that I might have the Bible in a language I can read. May every language group in the world be given access to Your Word in their "heart language."*

"God did not give the Bible so we could master him or it; God gave the Bible so we could live it, so we could be mastered by it. The moment we think we've mastered it, we have failed to be readers of the Bible." Pg. 52; McKnight, Scot. 2008. *The blue parakeet: rethinking how you read the Bible.* Grand Rapids, MI: Zondervan.

Psalms of Discipleship—Principle #21

Life Principles For Those Who Choose To Follow Jesus And Live The Discipled Life

Key Scripture: [1] How long, O LORD? Will You forget me forever? How long will You hide Your face from me? [2] How long shall I take counsel in my soul, *Having* sorrow in my heart all the day? How long will my enemy be exalted over me? [3] Consider *and* answer me, O LORD my God; Enlighten my eyes, or I will sleep the *sleep of* death, [4] And my enemy will say, "I have overcome him," *And* my adversaries will rejoice when I am shaken. **Psalm 13:1-4**

Core Value: Prayer

Why are we to pray? Christians are to pray because God has told them to do it. But in addition, God knows how much each believer needs to have a life bathed in prayer. Prayer is the conduit to one receiving answers to one's prayers. One must have confidence, not in what one is asking for, but confidence in the God one is asking to help (1 Jn. 5:14-15). The battle before the disciple is a serious one. Oswald Sanders reminds us that, "We are engaged in a relentless spiritual warfare that knows no truce. Our foes are unseen and intangible, but they are powerful. Against them only spiritual weapons will prevail . . . The fulcrum on which defeat or victory turns is our ability to pray aright and make intelligent use of our weapons. Jesus nowhere envisages His church in retreat" (Spiritual Discipleship 1994, p. 108).

God wants to answer the prayers of His children! One's prayer requests do not have to be a "wish list" for God to examine and forget about. The promise is sure: the disciple can have confidence in approaching God and ask Him for anything according to His will. He will hear the disciple's request and He will also give the disciple what they need. As one takes the step and mentors a person in prayer, it is important that one's confidence in God's ability to hear and answer prayers is conveyed to this person. The making of a quality disciple always is framed by confidence in God's wonderful promises revealed in His perfect Word.

Principle #21 & Personal Application: Quality disciples will pray, even though the circumstances of life are crushing.

- There is a commitment to pray even when it seems God has forgotten us.
- There is a commitment to pray even when there is great sorrow in our heart.
- There is a commitment to pray even when it seems the enemy is winning.
- There is a commitment to pray even when it seems the enemy is gloating.
- There is a commitment to pray knowing that unless God answers our prayer, we will perish.

Reflect & Respond: Some Really Good Questions To Ponder…

How do I convince myself to pray when it seems all hope is lost?

What is my approach to prayer when I am not getting an answer fast enough?

Prayer:

Lord Jesus, You have promised to never leave me or forsake me. You have promised me Your presence—even when I can't "see" You or "feel" You. May I not become impatient with You when my life circumstances are crushing me. May those same circumstances deepen instead my prayer relationship with You.

The Essential Core Values Of The Quality Disciple Are…
Grace—Worship—Bible Study—Prayer—Community—Service—Evangelism

Psalms of Discipleship—Principle #22

Life Principles For Those Who Choose To Follow Jesus And Live The Discipled Life

Key Scripture: [5] But I have trusted in Your lovingkindness; My heart shall rejoice in Your salvation. [6] I will sing to the LORD, Because He has dealt bountifully with me. **Psalm 13:5-6**

Core Value: Grace

Although the disciple of Jesus Christ often faces times of great adversity and spiritual challenge, it is God's grace that helps us not only survive, but to live in such a way where we actually grow in our faith. In the book, *Follow me: experience the loving leadership of Jesus*, Jan David Hettinga lends his voice to the perspective of grace being the catalyst to spiritual growth.

> "Grace, the supernatural forgiving love and transforming power of God, is released through the deliberate act of giving up the kingdom of self. Giving up is not a 'work.' It is a cessation of resistance. It is the losing wrestler surrendering to the winner. God repeatedly makes it clear that He resists the proud (those who are full of their own egoism) but gladly gives grace to the humble (Psalm 18:27, James 4:6-10, 1 Peter 5:5-6). The faucet that turns on the pipeline of saving grace is the voluntary choice of humility. This is the heart of repentance. The event of salvation then immediately becomes the process of humble obedience. And enabling grace keeps on flowing." (Hettinga 1996, pg. 141-142)

May His enabling grace keep on flowing through each one of us; every day, in every way.

Principle #22 & Personal Application: Quality disciples respond to the grace of God with trust, rejoicing, and singing.

Because God's grace has been bountifully applied to our lives:

- We can put our trust in His lovingkindess.
- We can rejoice in His salvation with our heart.
- We can with sing with a heart of praise and worship to the Lord.

[5] Many, O LORD my God, are the wonders which You have done, And Your thoughts toward us; There is none to compare with You. If I would declare and speak of them, They would be too numerous to count. **Psalms 40:5 (NASB95)**

Reflect & Respond: Some Really Good Questions To Ponder…

When I take a few moments and meditate on the grace of God, what comes to my mind?

How does the grace of God compel me to serve Him today?

Prayer:
Lord Jesus, You have dealt bountifully with me. You have given me what I do not deserve (that's grace) and not given me what I do deserve (that's mercy). May I put my trust in Your lovingkindness; may my heart rejoice in Your great salvation; may I sing to You today with a heart of praise and worship to my Great God!

The Essential Core Values Of The Quality Disciple Are…
Grace—Worship—Bible Study—Prayer—Community—Service—Evangelism

Psalms of Discipleship—Principle #23

Life Principles For Those Who Choose To Follow Jesus And Live The Discipled Life

Key Scripture: [1] O LORD, who may abide in Your tent? Who may dwell on Your holy hill? [2] He who walks with integrity, and works righteousness, And speaks truth in his heart. [3] He does not slander with his tongue, Nor does evil to his neighbor, Nor takes up a reproach against his friend; [4] In whose eyes a reprobate is despised, But who honors those who fear the LORD; He swears to his own hurt and does not change; [5] He does not put out his money at interest, Nor does he take a bribe against the innocent. He who does these things will never be shaken. **Psalm 15:1-5**

Core Value: Community

Trust in relationships must be established for any community to be considered "safe." The goal of any community of Christians should be "an environment of grace." In his book, *Choose The Life: Exploring a Faith that Embraces Discipleship,* Bill Hull suggests that, "Trust is only present when the faith community experiences relationships of trust in an environment of grace" (2004, pg. 130).

> An environment of grace is a safe place in which people are encouraged to live out the dream God has for them. An environment of grace is where we are accepted for who we are. That doesn't mean we are not expected to grow and develop—quite the opposite. It is only when we sense acceptance that we will lower our defenses and walk in the light, admitting our needs and allowing others to help us. That is when we will "trust others with me." (Hull 2004, pg. 150)

Living in an environment of grace will always help us treat others with great respect. May we all do our part in creating a safe place where we are helped and where we help others grow closer to Jesus.

Principle #23 & Personal Application: Quality disciples treat others with great respect. He or she…

- Walks, works, and speaks in a way that treats others with great respect (vs. 2). Their *walk* (what they do) is consistent with their *talk* (what they claim to be).

61

- Treats others with great respect by using words that do not slander; by committing to a way of life that lavishes each neighbor with godly kindness, and by protecting the integrity of the friendship (vs. 3).
- Despises "the flagrant sinners (NLT) and gives honor to those who are faithful followers of the Lord" (vs. 4).
- Has made the conscious decision to treat others with great respect by never taking advantage of those who are innocent and weaker (vs. 4-5).
- Experiences stability in life because they treat others with great respect (vs. 5).

Reflect & Respond: Some Really Good Questions To Ponder...

Would those who know me best consider me to be a person who treats others with great respect? Who in my "community of family and friends" need to be affirmed by me?

Prayer:
Lord Jesus, I do not want to be Your disciple in name only. By Your grace, help me be the kind of person who treats others with great respect.

"It is neither wise nor scriptural to pursue God apart from the community of faith. Our individual expressions of faith must be joined to corporate worship with the body of Christ." Pg. 17; Thomas, Gary. 2000. *Sacred Pathways: discover your soul's path to God, first Zondervan edition.* Grand Rapids, MI: Zondervan.

Psalms of Discipleship—Principle #24

Life Principles For Those Who Choose To Follow Jesus And Live The Discipled Life

Key Scripture: [5] The LORD is the portion of my inheritance and my cup; You support my lot. [6] The lines have fallen to me in pleasant places; Indeed, my heritage is beautiful to me. **Psalm 16:5-6**

Core Value: Grace

There are two ways to accumulate riches: our way or God's way. Our way, the way of self, costs us much more than we can pay. Sure, we might be able to collect in the course of our life an abundance of possessions and superficial "honors" and fame and be considered by many people as a "winner" of the rat race. But really, what kind of disciple of Jesus wants to win that kind of race? Our way of gaining riches will always lead to a temporal, decaying outcome. God's way to riches is far different. It begins and ends with poverty.

"Blessed [i.e., fortunate or prosperous] are the poor [i.e., those who are not arrogant] in spirit, for theirs is the kingdom of heaven. **Matthew 5:3 (NASB95)**

Dallas Willard translates this verse "Blessed are the spiritual zeros—the spiritually bankrupt, deprived and deficient, the spiritual beggars, those without a wisp of 'religion'—when the kingdom of the heavens comes upon them." (The Divine Conspiracy, pg. 100)

This is the point: when we renounce the way of legalism, works, and performance and acknowledge our spiritual poverty, we open ourselves to the full benefits of grace. Then, and only then, will we fully appreciate the Lord as the Portion of our inheritance, the Provider of all our needs, the Person who graces us with a beautiful life.

Principle #24 & Personal Application: Quality disciples are *so* blessed because of God's grace.

- The Lord is the *Portion* of our inheritance. It is grace that gives us what we do not *deserve*.

- The Lord is the *Provider* of all our needs. It is grace that gives us what we *need*.
- The Lord is the *Person* who graces us with a beautiful life. It is grace that gives us a life of *meaning* and *beauty*.

Reflect & Respond: Some Really Good Questions To Ponder...

What comes to my mind when I think about the ways God has been good to me?

As other people look at my life, can they see evidence of the grace of God at work in me?

Prayer:

Lord Jesus, thank You for being my Portion; my Provider; and the Person who graces me with a beautiful life. You, Lord Jesus, are the portion of my inheritance and my cup. You, Lord Jesus, are everything to me. May You, Lord Jesus, pour out Your all sufficient grace upon me.

The Essential Core Values Of The Quality Disciple Are...
Grace—Worship—Bible Study—Prayer—Community—Service—Evangelism

Psalms of Discipleship—Principle #25

Life Principles For Those Who Choose To Follow Jesus And Live The Discipled Life

Key Scripture: [7] I will bless the LORD who has counseled me; Indeed, my mind instructs me in the night. [8] I have set the LORD continually before me; Because He is at my right hand, I will not be shaken. **Psalm 16:7-8**

Core Value: Worship

Worship, true worship, is always an interactive act of faith. God moves and overwhelms the heart and we, the disciple of Jesus, respond accordingly with a fresh sense of awe, wonder, and love for God. Biblical worship must never been seen as a passive, religious duty. Worship is all about cultivating one's relationship with God. In their groundbreaking book, How People Grow, Cloud and Townsend offer this fresh and freeing perspective:

"Relationship is always more important than task. . . . Activity is bad when it takes the place of relationship rather than serving the purposes of relationship. Activity was designed by God to involve us in the work of life, not to replace closeness." (Pg. 342)

May we never confuse the kind of activity that keeps us busy doing religious duties (this is driven by works and performance for Him) but leaves us far and away from experiencing an intimacy with the Lord (this is driven by grace and acceptance by Him).

Principle #25 & Personal Application: Quality disciples, with a heart of worship, have a laser-like focus upon the Lord.

- A heart of worship causes the believer to bless the Lord.
- A heart of worship keeps the Lord continually before the believer.
- A heart of worship takes great comfort in experiencing the Lord's abiding presence.

Reflect & Respond: Some Really Good Questions To Ponder...

Is my worship of the Lord a transforming experience?

What do I need to do today in order to keep the Lord as the focal point of my mind?

Prayer:

Lord Jesus, as an act of faith, I choose to bless You. Thank You for the counsel You lavish upon me. What a joy it is for me to always be learning more about You and of Your great love for me. By faith, and out of a desire to walk closer with You, I choose to set You continually before me. Because You are at my right hand, I will not be shaken. I will bask in Your presence as I worship You. May my life be a testimony of one who is intently focused upon You.

"A. W. Tozer warns, 'The whole transaction of religious conversion has been made mechanical and spiritless. We have almost forgotten that God is a person and, as such, can be cultivated as any person can.'" Pg. 14; Thomas, Gary. 2000. *Sacred Pathways: discover your soul's path to God, first Zondervan edition.* Grand Rapids, MI: Zondervan.

Psalms of Discipleship—Principle #26

Life Principles For Those Who Choose To Follow Jesus And Live The Discipled Life

Key Scripture: You will make known to me the path of life; In Your presence is fullness of joy; In Your right hand there are pleasures forever. **Psalm 16:11**

Core Value: Grace

Everyone makes choices, even when it comes to how one lives the Christian life. We can do it our way (the way of performance and works) and quickly discover our way is never good enough; never satisfying enough; never right for us. Or we can do it God's way (the way of grace) and become overwhelmed with gratitude for His perfect direction, His abiding presence, and His abundant provision for us. In his classic book, Spiritual Theology, theologian Simon Chan states:

> "Modern Christians are not lacking in 'relevance.' What they do lack is a disciplined life and a critical mind to resist the temptation to conform to what everybody thinks or does (Rom 12:1-3). What they sorely need is an in-depth spiritual renewal of the whole person in order to decide for God or for the world. Decisiveness is the mark of true discipleship. 'If anyone would come after me, he must deny himself and take up his cross and follow me' (Mt 16:24). There is no 'middle ground,' according to Calvin: 'either the world must become worthless to us or hold us bound by intemperate love of it.'" (Pg. 69)

May the Lord pour out His all sufficient grace upon us as we make our choices and follow Jesus.

Principle #26 & Personal Application: Quality disciples experience a fulfilled life marked by the grace of God.

- Because of the grace of God, the quality disciple discovers one's purpose in life. The Lord will make known to *me* the path of life.
- Because of the grace of God, the quality disciple experiences full joy on life's path. The Lord will allow *me* to know fullness of joy in His presence.

- Because of the grace of God, the quality disciple rests in the Lord's perfect provision. The Lord's right hand contains *everything* that I will ever need.

Reflect & Respond: Some Really Good Questions To Ponder...

How can I be certain that the Lord has me on the right path of life?

What descriptive words come to my mind when I experience fullness of joy as I abide in the presence of the Lord?

Prayer:

Lord Jesus, what grace You pour out upon me! Thank You for the grace that makes me to know the path of life for me. Thank You for the grace that allows me to experience fullness of joy as I abide in Your presence. Thank You for providing for me everything that I need in this life. Lord Jesus, in Your right hand there are pleasures forever. Thank You that I do not have to look to anyone else or anything else to give me what I need.

"Once we accept the seldom-announced fact that we have nothing to give God or impress God with that will prompt Him to credit righteousness to our account, we will be ready to take His free gift." Pg. 23; Swindoll, Charles, R. 2003. *The Grace Awakening.* Nashville, TN: W Publishing Group.

Psalms of Discipleship—Principle #27

Life Principles For Those Who Choose To Follow Jesus And Live The Discipled Life

Key Scripture: I have called upon You, for You will answer me, O God; Incline Your ear to me, hear my speech. **Psalm 17:6**

Core Value: Prayer

One of the most successful marketing campaigns in recent years was the "got milk?" question that confronted us via billboards, magazines, and television commercials. Using a celebrity with a mustache of milk, the intention of the marketing company was to make sure that milk stayed on the forefront of our mind. It worked. Jeff Manning, the creative genius behind "got milk?", wanted to boost a struggling milk industry in California. The campaign not only turned around slumping milk sales, but it changed the face of consumer marketing forever. In some ways, many of us need to ask the question, "got prayer?" We know it is good for us. When we have tasted it, we usually desire more. We know it is good for us and we like the taste of it and the benefit it brings, but why is it that consistent, meaningful prayer is such a challenge for the disciple? Maybe we have a hard time believing that God really does listen to us, even in the ordinary affairs of life. Richard Foster expounds upon this when he writes,

> "To believe that God can reach us and bless us in the ordinary junctures of daily life is the stuff of prayer. But we want to throw this away, so hard is it for us to believe that God would enter our space. . . . the only place God can bless us is right where we are, because that is the only place we are!" (Prayer, Pg. 11)

It is time for a fresh "campaign" for "got prayer?" It is a campaign that reminds each one of us that even though our prayer lives might be in a slump, all it takes is a belief that prayer not only works, but it works well. Why does it work well? Prayer is personal. Prayer is expectant. Prayer is specific. In other words, God wants to enter our space. Will we let him in?

Principle #27 & Personal Application: Quality disciples cry out in prayer to a God who will not only *listen* but also *answer.*

- The prayer of a disciple of Jesus Christ is a *personal* one: "*I* have called upon You."
- The prayer of a disciple of Jesus Christ is an *expectant* one: "For *You will answer me*, O God."
- The prayer of a disciple of Jesus Christ is a *specific* one: "Incline Your ear to me, *hear my speech*."

Reflect & Respond: Some Really Good Questions To Ponder...

How can I ensure that my prayer life will be driven by my relationship with the Lord and not fall into a meaningless routine of activity?

When I talk to God in prayer, how can I be certain that I am hearing His voice?

Prayer:
     Lord Jesus, it is by faith, and faith alone, that I can cry out to You in prayer. I cannot "see" You, but I can sense Your presence. I cannot "touch" You, but I feel Your comforting arms around me. I cannot "hear" an audible voice, but I know the voice of the Shepherd in my heart. What a joy it is for me to know that when I do pray to You, You will answer me. Thank You O God for inclining Your ear to me and hearing my heart— for hearing the words that are spoken out loud and for hearing the words that remain hidden in my heart.

The Essential Core Values Of The Quality Disciple Are...
Grace—Worship—Bible Study—Prayer—Community—Service—Evangelism

Psalms of Discipleship—Principle #28

Life Principles For Those Who Choose To Follow Jesus And Live The Discipled Life

Key Scripture: Keep me as the apple of the eye; Hide me in the shadow of Your wings. **Psalm 17:8**

Core Value: Grace

How does it make you feel when someone considers you to be "special?" When you are made to feel special, there are certain words that describe what you might feel: "liked", received, believed in, accepted, treasured, cherished, seen as precious, prized, loved, valued. These are the kinds of words, when personally experienced, which give warmth to the heart and comfort in the soul. John Cloud and Henry Townsend (How People Grow) speak of the power of acceptance to the disciple of Jesus:

> "When we finally understand that God isn't mad at us anymore, we become free to concentrate on love and growth instead of trying to appease him." Pg. 147

> "What is acceptance, and why is it necessary in order for people to grow? The Bible teaches that acceptance begins with God: 'Accept one another, then, just as Christ accepted you, in order to bring praise to God.' (Rom. 15:7). Christ's acceptance of us is the model for how we are to accept each other.". . . . "It (acceptance) is closely related to grace, underserved merit. Acceptance is the result of the working of grace. Because of God's grace, we are accepted into relationship." Pg. 149

May we all experience what it means to be accepted by God and then begin to extend that acceptance to others too.

Principle #28 & Personal Application: Quality disciples take great delight in being one of God's prized possessions.

- It is because of the grace of God that we can be considered as a treasure to God.
- It is because of the grace of God that our personal value is not based upon *what* we are but upon *whose* we are.

- It is because of the grace of God that our security, our protection is in Him, hidden in the shadow of His wings.

Reflect & Respond: Some Really Good Questions To Ponder…

If God and I were to gaze into a mirror together, what precious qualities would He see in me?

Is there anything in my mind that prevents me from seeing me as God sees me?

Prayer:
 Lord Jesus, it is true. You do love and value me. You consider me to be the apple of Your eye. I am a treasure to You. What marvelous grace has been given me; that while I was still a sinner, You died for me (Romans 5:8). As I journey in this life I can rest in the comfort of Your care for me.

"We are wise to think of grace as a privilege to be enjoyed and protected, not a license to please ourselves." Pg. 125; Swindoll, Charles, R. 2003. *The Grace Awakening.* Nashville, TN: W Publishing Group.

Psalms of Discipleship—Principle #29

Life Principles For Those Who Choose To Follow Jesus And Live The Discipled Life

Key Scripture: [1] "I love You, O LORD, my strength." [2] The LORD is my rock and my fortress and my deliverer, My God, my rock, in whom I take refuge; My shield and the horn of my salvation, my stronghold. [3] I call upon the LORD, who is worthy to be praised, And I am saved from my enemies. **Psalm 18:1-3**

Core Value: Worship

A heart that has been touched by the power and presence of Almighty God will lead to an authentic worship of the Lord. Worship is the logical response of a needy person to a God who is not only great, but good too. Biblical worship is always focused upon His character and His awesome power. A disciple of Jesus desires to grow beyond a superficial worship into a life that is a living and holy sacrifice:

[1] Therefore I urge you, brethren, by the mercies of God, to present your bodies a living and holy sacrifice, acceptable to God, *which is* your spiritual service of worship. [2] And do not be conformed to this world, but be transformed by the renewing of your mind, so that you may prove what the will of God is, that which is good and acceptable and perfect. **Romans 12:1-2 (NASB95)**

In the book, Celebration of Discipline, Richard Foster underscores the priority of this kind of worship when he writes,

> "If the Lord is to be *Lord*, worship must have priority in our lives. The *first* commandment of Jesus is, 'Love the Lord your God with all your heart, and with all your soul, and with all your mind, and with all your strength' (Mark 12:30). The divine priority is worship first, service second. Our lives are to be punctuated with praise, thanksgiving, and adoration. Service flows out of worship. Service as a substitute for worship is idolatry. Activity is the enemy of adoration." (Pg. 160-161)

Principle #29 & Personal Application: Quality disciples offer a dynamic worship of the Lord from a heart that knows Him personally: He is mine!

As a believer:

- I can have a loving relationship with God (vs.1).
- I can personally experience a life that is impacted by Him: He is *my* strength, He is *my* rock, He is *my* fortress, He is *my* deliverer, He is *my* God, He is *my* refuge, He is *my* shield, He is the horn of *my* salvation, He is *my* stronghold (vs. 2).
- I can call upon the Lord who is worthy to be praised (vs. 3).
- I can be saved from my enemies (vs. 3).

Reflect & Respond: Some Really Good Questions To Ponder...

How can I make sure that my relationship with the Lord is personal and not distant and far removed?

In what ways does my prayer life complement my worship of God?

Prayer:

Lord Jesus, how amazing it is to love and follow You! To walk with You gives me such an assurance that You will be my strength, rock, fortress, deliverer, God, refuge, shield, horn of my salvation, and my stronghold. By faith, I call upon You for You are worthy to be praised!

The Essential Core Values Of The Quality Disciple Are...
Grace—Worship—Bible Study—Prayer—Community—Service—Evangelism

Psalms of Discipleship—Principle #30

Life Principles For Those Who Choose To Follow Jesus And Live The Discipled Life

Key Scripture: In my distress I called upon the LORD, And cried to my God for help; He heard my voice out of His temple, And my cry for help before Him came into His ears. **Psalm 18:6**

Core Value: Prayer

When the disciple of Jesus decides to follow Him, we are given no promises of a problem-free life. In fact, it seems the stronger commitment to Jesus can often lead to greater challenges to one's faith. To illustrate the point, there is a verse in Scripture that few desire to high-light with their marker and claim the promise of "Indeed, all who desire to live godly in Christ Jesus will be persecuted." **2 Timothy 3:12**

The quality of one's prayer life and relationship with the Lord is often tested in the crucible of desperation. In the book Good to Great in God's eyes: 10 Practices Great Christians Have in Common, Chip Ingram reminds us of how special prayer is to the Christian believer:

"Not only are great prayers deeply personal, they are also birthed in brokenness. When we come to God with a sense of bankruptcy, knowing we're in a desperate situation and have no resources to get ourselves out of it, God pays special attention. Brokenness will cause us to pour out our heart to God rather than trying to find the right words or the most persuasive arguments to present to him." Pg. 103

"Great prayers take God seriously . . . People who pray great prayers actually think God means what he says. Their prayers are promised centered, not problem centered. Because God is sovereign, omniscient, always good, and unable to lie, when he says he'll do something, he will. Great prayers take the person, the program, and the promises of God seriously." Pg. 107

Principle #30 & Personal Application: Quality disciples do not hesitate to cry out to God for help.

- The disciple of Jesus Christ embraces prayer during times of distress.

- The disciple of Jesus Christ knows where to direct his or her prayer: to the Lord.
- The disciple of Jesus Christ is not too proud to call for help.
- The disciple of Jesus Christ fully expects God to hear his or her cry for help.

Reflect & Respond: Some Really Good Questions To Ponder...

Has it been my history to use prayer only during an "emergency"?

When I offer my prayers to God, how confident am I in knowing that He will listen to my heart?

Prayer:

Lord Jesus, You are always a prayer away. Forgive me for the times when I only come to You during a time of distress. Continue to teach me why I can come to You: it is because of Your sacrificial love for me. May our relationship not be founded upon "convenience" but may my prayers to You develop within me a heart of love and devotion to You—both in the good times as well in times of great distress.

The Essential Core Values Of The Quality Disciple Are...
Grace—Worship—Bible Study—Prayer—Community—Service—Evangelism

Psalms of Discipleship—Principle #31

Life Principles For Those Who Choose To Follow Jesus And Live The Discipled Life

Key Scripture: As for God, His way is blameless; The word of the LORD is tried; He is a shield to all who take refuge in Him. **Psalm 18:30**

Core Value: Bible Study

We live in a day and time where there seems to be no "absolutes" but a whole lot of suggestions to choose whatever seems to feel right. It is an age of uncertainty. It is a culture in which we live that has lost its moral anchor. As disciples of Jesus, we believe that there are absolutes that govern how we should live and how we are to treat others and how we are to love God. We believe that the Scriptures clearly address everything the believer needs to know in order to live out the Christian life. But unless we miss the most important point, we need to make certain that we are growing in our relationship with the God of the Bible. In The Blue Parakeet, Scot McKnight offers these helpful thoughts:

"Believing in inspiration, revelation, infallibility or inerrancy, and authority describes one's *view* of the Bible. Fine. We need to talk about our view of the Bible. But that isn't enough. We have too many today who say, 'Now that you've got the right view of the Bible, you're on the right side of the angels.' Having the right view of the Bible isn't the point of the Bible. We need to have not only a 'view' of the Bible but also a 'relationship' to the God of the Bible." Pg. 95

Principle #31 & Personal Application: Quality disciples find great comfort and joy in the Word of God.

- We find great comfort and joy *knowing* that our God is perfect and His promises are true.
- We find great comfort and joy *knowing* that our God is our perfect guide, showing us the way to safety in Him.
- We find great comfort and joy *knowing* that our God has provided for us a perfect book, a perfect living Word that we can rest our lives upon with great abandon.

[12] For the word of God is living and active and sharper than any two-edged sword, and piercing as far as the division of soul and spirit, of both joints and marrow, and able to judge the thoughts and intentions of the heart.
Hebrews 4:12 (NASB95)

Reflect & Respond: Some Really Good Questions To Ponder...

When I read from God's Word, do I just look for the things that I like, or do I carefully read and listen to what God is saying to me?

When and where was the last time God has spoken to me from His Word, giving me great comfort and joy?

Prayer:
Lord Jesus, I celebrate the fact that You are my God and that Your way is always perfect and blameless. I celebrate that Your Word is always true, never misleading me, always helping me to find my way to a safe refuge in You. I celebrate the comfort and joy I receive as I read your Word and apply it to my life.

"A learning of the Word of God can be validated only by a transformed life . . . The only teaching that can be rightly called 'Bible teaching' focuses, not on processing information, but on hearing and responding to God's own loving voice.'" Pg. 70 [cited Larry Richards, 'Church Teaching: Content Without Context,' *Christianity Today*, 15 April 1977, p. 16]; McQuilkin, Robertson. 1992. *Understanding and applying the Bible*, Chicago, IL: Moody Press.

Psalms of Discipleship—Principle #32

Life Principles For Those Who Choose To Follow Jesus And Live The Discipled Life

Key Scripture: [35] You have also given me the shield of Your salvation, And Your right hand upholds me; And Your gentleness makes me great. [36] You enlarge my steps under me, And my feet have not slipped. **Psalm 18:35-36**

Core Value: Grace

God does not give grace to us so we may rest on our own spiritual laurels and coast into a heavenly bliss after this life. God, by His grace, has called us to respond to grace by doing great things for God. In his book, "Good to Great in God's Eyes," Chip Ingram makes this excellent point:

> "Good Christians live the Christian life. They love God, walk in integrity, demonstrate faithfulness to their mates, spend time in the Bible because they want to hear from God, make the effort to discover their spiritual gifts, use those gifts in their local church, give their tithes and offerings, go on missions trips, and help their kids grow up to be godly men and women. They do what God calls them to do, and they serve him well. Great Christians, on the other hand, do all that and then pass it on. You can be a good Christian by obeying God and loving people, but if you haven't poured your life into others, your life ends with a period. Great Christians end with a comma. They live the life of faith in a way that takes God's grace to them and imparts it into the lives of others. They multiply themselves again and again. Good Christians 'live the life'; great Christians 'leave a legacy.'" Pg. 189

What kind of legacy are you leaving behind: a period, or a comma?

Principle #32 & Personal Application: Quality disciples are sobered by God's all-consuming grace.

It is the all-consuming grace of God that
- gives us the shield, the protection, of His salvation.
- upholds us with His right hand of strength and provision.
- makes us great through His gentleness towards us.

- makes our steps of faith sure and firm in Him.

For if, by the trespass of the one man, death reigned through that one man, how much more will those who receive <u>God's abundant provision of grace</u> and of the gift of righteousness reign in life through the one man, Jesus Christ. **Romans 5:17 (NIV)**

Reflect & Respond: Some Really Good Questions To Ponder...

When I reflect upon God's all-consuming grace in *my life*, what kinds of images come to mind?

In what areas of my life—today—do I need to apply God's all-consuming grace?

Prayer:

Lord Jesus, now, more than ever before, I need to be a person of grace: living by it, experiencing it, sharing it, being consumed by it.

The Essential Core Values Of The Quality Disciple Are...
Grace—Worship—Bible Study—Prayer—Community—Service—Evangelism

Psalms of Discipleship—Principle #33

Life Principles For Those Who Choose To Follow Jesus And Live The Discipled Life

Key Scripture: The LORD lives, and blessed be my rock; And exalted be the God of my salvation, **Psalm 18:46**

Core Value: Worship

Do you have a contagious worship of God that leads others into His presence too? If we are ever going to make a difference in making disciples who become disciple makers for Jesus, we must all become "worship leaders." We are not saying anything about singing on a stage in a church building. We are saying our worship of God must be authentic, real and meaningful to us first before we can lead anyone else into a deeper relationship with Jesus. Henry and Richard Blackaby remind us of this truth:

> "One of the issues regarding spiritual leadership is whether spiritual leaders can take people to places they themselves have never been. That depends on one's definition of spiritual leadership. If spiritual leadership is understood as taking people to a *location* or completing a *task*, then leaders can lead people to places they have never been. But if the goal of leadership is a *relationship*, then leaders will never move their people beyond where they have gone themselves. Leaders can lead people to relocate their organization or to build a building or to grow in size without prior experience in these areas. But leaders cannot take their people into a relationship with Christ that goes any deeper than they have gone themselves. Followers may grow deeper spiritually in spite of their spiritually immature leaders, but they will not grow deeper because of such people. Thus, spiritual leaders must continually be growing themselves if they are to lead their people into a mature, intimate relationship with Christ. Leaders will not lead their people to higher levels of prayer unless they have already ascended to those heights themselves. Leaders will not lead others to deeper levels of trust in God unless they have a mature faith themselves." Spiritual Leadership. Pg. 128

Who are you leading, where are you taking them, and what are they experiencing along the way?

Principle #33 & Personal Application: Quality disciples have a keen awareness of the greatness of God.

- We know our God is great because He lives!
- We know our God is great because He is our Rock!
- We know our God is great because He is the God of our salvation!
- We know our God is great because He is the Everlasting God, the LORD, the Creator of the ends of the earth, the sovereign King and Sustainer of the Universe!
- We know our God is great because He really does care for us!

[28] Do you not know? Have you not heard? The Everlasting God, the LORD, the Creator of the ends of the earth Does not become weary or tired. His understanding is inscrutable. [29] He gives strength to the weary, And to *him who* lacks might He increases power. [30] Though youths grow weary and tired, And vigorous young men stumble badly, [31] Yet those who wait for the LORD Will gain new strength; They will mount up *with* wings like eagles, They will run and not get tired, They will walk and not become weary. **Isaiah 40:28-31 (NASB95)**

Reflect & Respond: Some Really Good Questions To Ponder…

How will my worship of God be enhanced if I begin to focus upon the Living Savior?

When I begin to meditate upon the greatness of God, what kinds of thoughts fill my mind?

Prayer:

   Lord Jesus, help me live in the reality that I am loving and serving a Living Savior. I bless You, for You are my Rock. I exalt You, for You are the God of my salvation. May I become a contagious worship leader so that others may worship You too.

Psalms of Discipleship—Principle #34

Life Principles For Those Who Choose To Follow Jesus And Live The Discipled Life

Key Scripture: The heavens are telling of the glory of God; And their expanse is declaring the work of His hands. **Psalm 19:1**

Core Value: Worship

Disciples of Jesus Christ are given a privileged "front row seat" as we gaze at the nighttime sky. We've all done it: on a cloudless night where there is little man-made light that distracts from the glow of heaven's lights consisting of the moon and countless stars that make up our cosmic neighborhood called the Milky Way, we look; we stare; we are overcome by our smallness and His greatness. We are in awe of God's glory. How can it be that the same God who created all of this heavenly landscape by the work of His hands can also have an intimate love-relationship with us? If we are not careful, we can begin to over analyze this question and fail to do what is necessary, which is to worship God. In the book, Celebration of Discipline, Richard Foster reminds us that,

> "Worship is something we do. Studying the theology of worship and debating the forms of worship are all good, but by themselves they are inadequate. In the final analysis we learn to worship by worshiping." Pg. 170

May the Lord grant us the grace to look beyond our inward self and to set our gaze on His majestic glory and worship Him.

Principle #34 & Personal Application: Quality disciples are struck by the wonder of God's marvelous creation.

- It is a wonder to know that God has put in place, in the heavens, a creation that knows its place: to tell of the glory of God.
- It is a wonder to know that God has placed His fingerprints on His creation.
- It is a wonder to know that God receives all glory from His creation.

O LORD, our Lord, How majestic is Your name in all the earth, Who have displayed Your splendor above the heavens! **Psalm 8:1 (NASB95)**

[3] When I consider Your heavens, the work of Your fingers, The moon and the stars, which You have ordained; [4] What is man that You take thought of him, And the son of man that You care for him? [5] Yet You have made him a little lower than God, And You crown him with glory and majesty! **Psalm 8:3-5 (NASB95)**

Reflect & Respond: Some Really Good Questions To Ponder…

When is the last time I was really struck by and in awe of God's creation?

What kinds of steps can I begin to take that will give me a better appreciation of God's creation?

Prayer:

Lord Jesus, the heavens do tell of the glory of God. As I gaze at Your creation, I worship You. May I never take for granted the wonder of what You have made. May I always be struck by the wonder of God's marvelous creation.

The Essential Core Values Of The Quality Disciple Are…
Grace—Worship—Bible Study—Prayer—Community—Service—Evangelism

Psalms of Discipleship—Principle #35

Life Principles For Those Who Choose To Follow Jesus And Live The Discipled Life

Key Scripture: [7] The law of the LORD is perfect, restoring the soul; The testimony of the LORD is sure, making wise the simple. [8] The precepts of the LORD are right, rejoicing the heart; The commandment of the LORD is pure, enlightening the eyes. [9] The fear of the LORD is clean, enduring forever; The judgments of the LORD are true; they are righteous altogether. [10] They are more desirable than gold, yes, than much fine gold; Sweeter also than honey and the drippings of the honeycomb. [11] Moreover, by them Your servant is warned; In keeping them there is great reward. **Psalm 19:7-11**

Core Value: Bible Study

Love letters. At one time we probably either wrote a love letter or received one, or both! Perhaps your first love letter was sent to your grammar school classmate, hoping that the encrypted code in the letter would be understood by a wink or a tender smile that communicates, "message received!" In a similar way, that is God's hope for us. He loves us and He has taken the risk with us by sending us a love letter with a clear, unencrypted, message that requires our response: will we love Him or ignore Him? There are many who read God's love letters (The Bible), have mastered its content, but have failed to become transformed by its message. The goal of the quality disciple should never be the accumulation of biblical facts for the sake of knowledge, but the personal *application* of those facts that lead to a transformed life. Robertson McQuilkin lends his perspective on this when he writes,

> "A learning of the Word of God can be validated only by a transformed life . . . The only teaching that can be rightly called 'Bible teaching' focuses, not on processing information, but on hearing and responding to God's own loving voice.'" Pg. 70 [cited Larry Richards, 'Church Teaching: Content Without Context,' *Christianity Today*, 15 April 1977, p. 16]. McQuilkin, Robertson. 1992. *Understanding and applying the Bible*, Chicago, IL: Moody Press.

Scot McKnight adds to the discussion of how we are to approach the Bible:

"God did not give the Bible so we could master him or it; God gave the Bible so we could live it, so we could be mastered by it. The moment we think we've mastered it, we have failed to be readers of the Bible." Pg. 52 (*The blue parakeet: rethinking how you read the Bible.* Grand Rapids, MI: Zondervan.

May we all fall in love with the Author of His love letters and be mastered by Him.

Principle #35 & Personal Application: Quality disciples have an unquenchable passion to *know* and *experience* the Word of God. When we intimately *know* and *experience* the Word of God…

- We believe that the Law of the Lord is perfect (blameless, whole, intact).
- We believe that the testimony of the Lord is sure (trustworthy, clear, consistent).
- We believe that the precepts of the Lord are right (straight).
- We believe that the commandment of the Lord is pure (clear, plain, radiant).
- We believe that the fear of the Lord is clean (pure, sacred).
- We believe that the judgments of the Lord are true (accurate, sure, correct)
- We believe that God's Word is more precious than gold, sweeter than honey.
- We believe that there is a great blessing for those who obey God's Word.

Reflect & Respond: Some Really Good Questions To Ponder…

What are some evidences in my life that show I really treasure my Bible?

How can I be sure that I do not read my Bible for the accumulation of facts alone?

Prayer:
Lord Jesus, May Your Word always be a treasure to my heart. I thank and praise You for a Bible that is perfect, sure, right, pure, clean, true, and more precious that gold and more sweeter than honey. As I apply and obey Your Word may I live a transformed life and experience great reward.

Psalms of Discipleship—Principle #36

Life Principles For Those Who Choose To Follow Jesus And Live The Discipled Life

Key Scripture: Let the words of my mouth and the meditation of my heart Be acceptable in Your sight, O LORD, my rock and my Redeemer. **Psalm 19:14**

Core Value: Worship

Worship can be an inward experience as well as an outward expression of the heart. Our worship of God can take on different kinds of forms. One form of worship is words. Words have meaning. Words are the windows that reveal what we seek to communicate. Words help us offer our worship to the Lord. The constant challenge for each disciple of Jesus is to make certain the words one is using (those that are spoken and those that are only thought) are acceptable to the Lord. Here are some questions that must be posed to the quality disciple: "does what I say aloud match what I am pondering upon in the deep recesses of my mind? Or have I succumbed to a life where what I say and think no longer has credibility?" When we make a commitment to have His words become our words, our worship of Him impacts every area of our life. Remember, worship is not just limited to what we do on a Sunday morning with other believers. Worship is a lifestyle. Brad Waggoner says this:

> "You know when you are around a leader who spends time meditating and reflecting on God's Word. During the times in my life when I am consistently in God's Word, it comes out my pores. You cannot keep it contained. It bleeds out into your thinking and into your conversations." Pg. 70 (Waggoner, Brad J. 2008. *The shape of faith to come: spiritual formation and the future of discipleship.* Nashville, TN: B&H Publishing Group.)

Michael Wilkins says,

> "Abiding in Jesus' words does not mean perpetual Bible study. Rather, it means to know and to live in what Jesus says about life. Instead of listening to the world's values, disciples must listen to what Jesus says." Pg. 357 (Wilkins, Michael J. 1992. *Following the Master:*

discipleship in the steps of Jesus. Grand Rapids, MI: Zondervan Publishing House.)

In other words, we listen to His Word, we think about it, and then we say it out loud.

Principle #36 & Personal Application: Quality disciples experience an authentic worship that is both verbal and non-verbal.

Using words that are acceptable to the Lord will help us worship the Lord in the way He desires:

- Authentic worship is personal as we "let" or open our life to the person and influence of Jesus Christ
- Authentic worship is spoken via the words of our mouth
- Authentic worship occurs in the deep recesses of our heart, meditating upon the greatness of our God
- Authentic worship is acceptable in the sight of the One who alone is worthy of our worship
- Authentic worship is directed to the Lord, our rock and our Redeemer

Reflect & Respond: Some Really Good Questions To Ponder...
What is it like for me to experience a conversation with God or with others after I have marinated my heart in God's Word?

How can my words become a catalyst for worship?

What do I spend most of my waking hours thinking about within the recesses of my heart?

Prayer:
Lord Jesus, like the psalmist, I too desire this to be true of me: Let the words of my mouth and the meditation of my heart be acceptable in Your sight, O Lord, my rock and my Redeemer.

Psalms of Discipleship—Principle #37

Life Principles For Those Who Choose To Follow Jesus And Live The Discipled Life

Key Scripture: May the LORD answer you in the day of trouble! May the name of the God of Jacob set you *securely* on high! **Psalm 20:1**

Core Value: Prayer

What is the purpose of prayer? Is prayer a "wish list" we deliver to God with the strict expectation that God will answer us with what we want—the complete satisfaction of our will? Or is Biblical prayer much more than a tool that makes us feel better when our circumstances are difficult? In his book "Prayer: Finding the Heart's True Home," Richard Foster offers these valuable insights on the familiar struggle between God's will and our own:

> "To applaud the will of God, to do the will of God, even to fight for the will of God is not difficult . . . until it comes at cross-purposes with our will. Then the lines are drawn, the debate begins, and the self-deception takes over. But in the school of Gethsemane we learn that 'my will, my way, my good, must yield to higher authority." Pg. 50

> "Struggle is important because the Prayer of Relinquishment is Christian prayer and not fatalism. We do not resign ourselves to fate . . . We are not locked into a preset, determinist future. Ours is an open, not a closed universe. We are 'co-laborers with God,' as the Apostle Paul put it—working with God to determine the outcome of events. Therefore our prayer efforts are a genuine give and take, a true dialogue with God—and a true struggle." Pg. 50-51

> "The fact that God speaks to us is no guarantee that we hear or understand correctly." Pg. 51

> "The Prayer of Relinquishment is a bona fide letting go, but it is a release with hope. We have no fatalistic resignation. We are buoyed up by a confident trust in the character of God. Even when all we see are the tangled threads on the backside of life's tapestry, we know that God is good and is out to do us good always. That gives us hope

to believe that we are the winners, regardless of what we are being called upon to relinquish. God is inviting us deeper in and higher up. There is training in righteousness, transforming power, new joys, deeper intimacy." Pg. 52

"Relinquishment brings us to a priceless treasure: the crucifixion of the will." Pg. 53

Yes, God will answer us in our time of trouble. And yes, He will deliver us in a way that gives Him the most glory. But prayer is much more than something that gets us out of trouble. In other words, prayer is a struggle that is well worth embracing. We discover that the process of prayer is far more important than getting the answers for which we were hoping. For it is through prayer we are allowed to gain a more intimate knowledge of the heart of God and of His abundant love for us.

Principle #37 & Personal Application: Quality disciples fully expect God to answer prayer His way and in His time in the crucible of crisis.

- The believer can take comfort when our prayers are directed to the Lord
- The believer can take comfort that the Lord will answer us in the day of trouble
- The believer can take comfort in the Lord's ability to deliver us because of His great name

Reflect & Respond: Some Really Good Questions To Ponder…

When is the last time that I can remember, where the Lord answered my prayer during a crisis?

The next time I find myself in the crucible of crisis, what kinds of things do I need to remember?

Prayer:

Lord Jesus, just because I have chosen to follow You does not exempt me from having to experience trials; in fact, it seems that since I have chosen to follow You, the trials have increased, not decreased. Nevertheless, I thank You that during my day of trouble You will answer me and deliver me because of Your great Name.

Psalms of Discipleship—Principle #38

Life Principles For Those Who Choose To Follow Jesus And Live The Discipled Life

Key Scripture: Some boast in chariots and some in horses, But we will boast in the name of the LORD, our God. **Psalm 20:7**

Core Value: Worship

No matter what kind of a culture one lives in, there will always be the inner pull to place one's trust in what one can see and touch. Even if we profess to be "Christians," we can be tempted into subtle forms of "idolatry." Years ago, as a horrific typhoon ripped through the Philippines, a photographer captured on film an image that illustrates perfectly what some people try to do: "save their idols." Four men, drenched with a mud-soaked rain, were heroically trying to prevent the destruction of a statue of Buddha, made of stone. In fact, this was the caption: "saving Buddha." This a true, but sad story. But before we scoff at their foolishness, how many of our own idols have we tried to save? Idols? Us? Is that even possible? Whenever we place our trust in something or someone else besides the Lord, we have stepped into the slippery slope of idolatry. Why would we want to seek to save something that cannot even save itself?

9 How foolish are those who manufacture idols. These prized objects are really worthless. The people who worship idols don't know this, so they are all put to shame. 10 Who but a fool would make his own god— an idol that cannot help him one bit? 11 All who worship idols will be disgraced along with all these craftsmen—mere humans— who claim they can make a god. They may all stand together, but they will stand in terror and shame. Isaiah 44:9-11 (NLT)

May the Lord save us from the idols of our own making.

Principle #38 & Personal Application: Quality disciples do not worship anything or anyone other than Jesus Christ.

- There are some who brag about what they have and wind up worshiping it

- There are some who brag about who they know and wind up worshiping them
- But there are some, those who are followers of Jesus Christ, who brag in the name of the One who is the Lord our God and wind up worshiping Him

The temptation to compromise and cheat our worship of God is constantly pounding upon the human heart. We have been taught by the world that it is all about us. We expect to have things the way we want them to be. We are frequently being pulled down as we seek to satisfy the cries of our fleshly desires. What are we—those who have been called to worship the Lord our God and serve Him only—to do? We are to have a consuming passion for Him.

Then Jesus said to his disciples, "If anyone would come after me, he must deny himself and take up his cross and follow me. For whoever wants to save his life will lose it, but whoever loses his life for me will find it. Matthew 16:24-25

Reflect & Respond: Some Really Good Questions To Ponder...

Have I allowed anything (my job, my material possessions, my time, my favorite hobby) to occupy the throne of my heart and replace the Kingship of Jesus?

Have I allowed anyone (my spouse, my family, my friends, my spiritual leader, my favorite sports star, my favorite musician, myself) to occupy the throne of my heart and replace the Kingship of Jesus?

Prayer:
Lord Jesus, on more than one occasion, I have allowed my heart to become overcome in a spiritual coup d'état. Forgive me when I put things and people above You. I would much rather put my abiding trust in the name of the Lord my God.

Psalms of Discipleship—Principle #39

Life Principles For Those Who Choose To Follow Jesus And Live The Discipled Life

Key Scripture: Save, O LORD; May the King answer us in the day we call. **Psalm 20:9**

Core Value: Community & Prayer

When is the last time you attended a prayer meeting where you sensed a special visitation from the Lord? You came to this meeting with a full heart—with an almost desperate expectation— that, unless God intervened, the burden would continue to crush your soul. And then, during the course of the meeting, joy invaded your heart and peace flooded your soul. God had met with you and your group. In biblical community, there is a comfort provided where you can draw upon others for strength. Together, the group can call out to the Lord and appeal to Him for His help. Yes, there are certain times when we need solitude and must enter the prayer closet alone. But there are also times when we are called to pray and do life together with other believers. We all need to belong to a community. Bill Hull does a good job of explaining the benefit for community when he writes,

"Character is shaped in community." Pg. 96

"I have come to believe that the primary and exclusive work of the church is spiritual transformation. That is about a change in which our character is being transformed into the image of Christ. And that character is formed in community, not in isolation. It is formed in the friction of living with others in covenant and then being tested in isolation. We lead out of our character even more than our skills." Pg. 129

"As the African proverb tells us, 'If you want to go fast, go alone. If you want to go far, go together" Pg. 107 Bill Hull, Choose the Life.

So, are you going fast . . . alone? Or have you decided to become a part of community and go far together?

Principle #39 & Personal Application: Quality disciples long to experience the power of corporate prayer.

- There is supernatural power when a group of believers cry out for His great salvation
- There is supernatural power when a group of believers fully expect the King to answer us in the day we call
- There is supernatural power when a group of believers meet to pray together

They were continually devoting themselves to the apostles' teaching and to fellowship, to the breaking of bread and to prayer. **Acts 2:42 (NASB95)**

[19] "Again I say to you, that if two of you agree on earth about anything that they may ask, it shall be done for them by My Father who is in heaven. [20] "For where two or three have gathered together in My name, I am there in their midst." **Matthew 18:19-20 (NASB95)**

Therefore, confess your sins to one another, and pray for one another so that you may be healed. The effective prayer of a righteous man can accomplish much. **James 5:16 (NASB95)**

And when they had prayed, the place where they had gathered together was shaken, and they were all filled with the Holy Spirit and *began* to speak the word of God with boldness. **Acts 4:31 (NASB95)**

Reflect & Respond: Some Really Good Questions To Ponder…

When I pray with others, what is my expectation?

When I pray with others, has my experience been typically fulfilling or empty?

Who would I consider to be my "prayer partners"?

When is the last time I prayed with my prayer partners?

Prayer:
>Lord Jesus, help me be faithful in prayer; especially with other believers.

Psalms of Discipleship—Principle #40

Life Principles For Those Who Choose To Follow Jesus And Live The Discipled Life

Key Scripture: Be exalted, O LORD, in Your strength; We will sing and praise Your power. **Psalm 21:13**

Core Value: Worship

Many of us who seek to follow Jesus Christ frequently experience the negative results of a hurried pace of life and fail to experience the intimacy of knowing Him. Our religious habits have trained us to know all of the right answers but we often lack the discipline (or faith) to apply what we know to be true. We all need to take a deep, cleansing breath and learn the art of being still before the Lord. Worship is the healing balm to a life that is overstretched and overwhelmed by the cares of this world. When our world is rocked by chaos, crisis, and change, what are we to do? Do we go into panic mode and forget our great God or do we apply His grace as we worship the Lord and place our trust in Him? Pastor and writer Mark Batterson shared this nugget of truth at the Catalyst Leadership Conference: "It is hard to be still . . . and just stand there and trust the Lord." The psalmist said it this way:

"Cease *striving* [or be still] and know that I am God; I will be exalted among the nations, I will be exalted in the earth." **Psalm 46:10 (NASB95)**

Grace allows us to be still, to cease striving and worship Him.

Principle #40 & Personal Application: Quality disciples have a heart to worship the One who is exalted and worthy of praise.

What does it mean to have a heart of worship?

- A heart of worship is set upon an exalted God
- A heart of worship is set upon a God who is strong
- A heart of worship is set upon a God who evokes singing and praise to the One who has all power

Reflect & Respond: Some Really Good Questions To Ponder...

When I set my heart upon the Lord, what kinds of emotions usually fill my mind?

What kinds of spiritual disciplines (for example: prayer, Bible study, fasting, journaling, solitude, etc.) help me to focus upon the Lord and worship Him?

What does it mean for me to exalt the Lord in His strength while I sing and praise His power?

Prayer:
Lord Jesus, often I am weak and failing. I need Your mercy and grace in abundance. Worship of You is my catalyst to spiritual growth. May my worship of You be empowered by Your strength and power. In faith, I will sing and praise Your power.

The Essential Core Values Of The Quality Disciple Are...
Grace—Worship—Bible Study—Prayer—Community—Service—Evangelism

Psalms of Discipleship—Principle #41

Life Principles For Those Who Choose To Follow Jesus And Live The Discipled Life

Key Scripture: All the ends of the earth will remember and turn to the LORD, And all the families of the nations will worship before You. **Psalm 22:27**

Core Value: Evangelism

As a believer, is your life "attractional?" In other words, does your life attract the people who have yet to experience the saving power of the gospel? As disciples of Jesus, we must seek to think like Him, to act like Him, to love like Him. In her foundational book on evangelism, Rebecca Pippert offers this clear and convincing challenge to those who desire to follow Jesus:

"If we are to be followers of Jesus, his values must permeate our values. We need to be concerned more with how our lives reflect his love, his holiness, his obedience, than with the latest witnessing techniques. When we live as Jesus did, in his power and with his presence, seekers will be drawn to us. Evangelism will not be a dreaded task to be ticked off every Wednesday. Rather, sharing Jesus will become a true delight and evangelism will become a lifestyle." (Pg. 102) Pippert, Rebecca Manley. 1979. *Out of the salt shaker and into the world*. Downers Grove, IL: InterVarsity Press.

Has evangelism become a "religious duty (a dreaded task)" or has it become a lifestyle for you? May our own love for the Lord of the Harvest give us the kind of lifestyle that will attract others to love and follow Him.

Principle #41 & Personal Application: Quality disciples have a heart for the Lord of the Harvest.

- The Lord of the Harvest will have an impact upon the whole world as people will remember Him and turn to Him
- The Lord of the Harvest will be the sole recipient of worship from all of the families of nations
- The Lord of the Harvest seeks out laborers who will join Him for the great harvest of souls who need Jesus Christ

97

[36] Seeing the people, He felt compassion for them, because they were distressed and dispirited like sheep without a shepherd. [37] Then He said* to His disciples, "The harvest is plentiful, but the workers are few. [38] "Therefore beseech the Lord of the harvest to send out workers into His harvest." **Matthew 9:36-38 (NASB95)**

"Do you not say, 'There are yet four months, and *then* comes the harvest'? Behold, I say to you, lift up your eyes and look on the fields, that they are white for harvest. **John 4:35 (NASB95)**

Reflect & Respond: Some Really Good Questions To Ponder...

Who is in my immediate circle of family and friends who is lost without Christ?

What kinds of practical things can I begin to do that will allow me to share the Gospel in a way that will be clear and convincing to my lost family and friends?

Prayer:

Lord Jesus, You are the Lord of the Harvest. You have already told me that the fields are white unto harvest and that the laborers are few. Please Lord, add me to Your team of laborers and thrust me into Your harvest. May many souls come to know You because of the power of Your Gospel that is at work within me.

Psalms of Discipleship—Principle #42

Life Principles For Those Who Choose To Follow Jesus And Live The Discipled Life

Key Scripture: The LORD is my shepherd, I shall not want. **Psalm 23:1 [NASB95]** or "Because the Lord is my Shepherd, I have everything that I need." **[The Living Bible]**

Core Value: Grace

Do we really know what it means to have God, the Shepherd of the 23rd Psalm take care of us? The prevailing view in our culture demands that each one of us be independent, self-providing, self-protecting. . . . self, self, self. How well has that strategy done for you? After the Fall in the Garden, there became a seismic paradigm shift on the role mankind began to assume. Instead of God serving as the catalyst for life, we reversed the roles. Mankind sought to exchange roles with the Creator God. We want control, all of it. We want to provide, everything. We want to set the rules, and live by them. We need a Shepherd who will do these things for us. May each one of us long for the care of the Shepherd of the 23rd Psalm.

Principle #42 & Personal Application: Quality disciples lack for nothing because the Lord has provided everything that is needed.

- It is grace that allows me to know that the Lord is my shepherd.
- It is grace that allows me to know that the Lord provides all of my needs.
- It is grace that allows me to know that worry and anxiety has no place in my heart because "the Lord is my Shepherd, I have everything I need!" **Psalms 23:1 (TLB)**

Like a shepherd He will tend His flock, In His arm He will gather the lambs And carry *them* in His bosom; He will gently lead the nursing *ewes*. **Isaiah 40:11 (NASB95)**

I would love to tell you what I think of Jesus. Since I found in Him a friend so strong and true; I would tell you how he changed my life completely, He did something that no other friend could do.

CHORUS: No one ever cared for me like Jesus, There's no other friend so kind as He; No one else could take the sin and darkness from me, O', how much He cared for me. (Written by Charles Weigle. Public Domain)

Reflect & Respond: Some Really Good Questions To Ponder...

What does it really mean for me to have Jesus, the Great Shepherd, care for me?

What types of things *do I let Him care for* and what kinds of things *do I not allow Him to take care of* for me?

Prayer:

Lord Jesus, far too many times I seek to be my own shepherd. Today, I want You to be my Shepherd. Please, O Lord, take care of me.

The Essential Core Values Of The Quality Disciple Are...
Grace—Worship—Bible Study—Prayer—Community—Service—Evangelism

Psalms of Discipleship—Principle #43

Life Principles For Those Who Choose To Follow Jesus And Live The Discipled Life

Key Scripture: He makes me lie down in green pastures; He leads me beside quiet waters. **Psalm 23:2**

Core Value: Grace

One of the negative tenets of our western culture is the mistaken belief that we must work harder than God in taking care of our spiritual needs. We think if we pray more, study more, fast more, share more, and serve more, we will become more "spiritual." Well, the Pharisees did that too and we know where that got them. Yes, there is a place for the believer to work on spiritual disciplines; but they are only the means to an end. The end goal for the disciple of Jesus is to have a closer relationship with Him and this goal is only fulfilled when we take the pathway of grace. In his book, *Follow me: experience the loving leadership of Jesus,* Jan David Hettinga writes:

"Grace, the supernatural forgiving love and transforming power of God, is released through the deliberate act of giving up the kingdom of self. Giving up is not a 'work.' It is a cessation of resistance. It is the losing wrestler surrendering to the winner. God repeatedly makes it clear that He resists the proud (those who are full of their own egoism) but gladly gives grace to the humble (Psalm 18:27, James 4:6-10, 1 Peter 5:5-6). The faucet that turns on the pipeline of saving grace is the voluntary choice of humility. This is the heart of repentance. The event of salvation then immediately becomes the process of humble obedience. And enabling grace keeps on flowing." Pg. 141-142

"Submission is an event, and then a *lifetime process*. Once we start kingdom living, we must keep submitting our wills to our King. That's what repentance means—turning from our way to God's way, as a *lifestyle*. When we stop repenting we start regressing. The reason this happens seems elusive but it isn't. When we stop humbling ourselves, we shut off the free flow of the supernatural ability that God calls grace." Pg. 182

The Shepherd wants us to lie down our will and submit to His. The Lord seeks to lead us away from chaos and turmoil into a place of inner rest. May

God give us the heart to accept His grace as we rest in His abundant provision and restful peace.

Principle #43 & Personal Application: Quality disciples experience the blessing of abundant provision and restful peace when they submit their will to God.

- Grace allows the disciple to experience God's best
- Grace moves the human heart to stop fighting for "my way" and to lie down into His green pastures of rich and abundant provision
- Grace moves the human heart to stop fighting for "my way" and to allow Him to lead me beside His quiet waters of peace and security

Reflect & Respond: Some Really Good Questions To Ponder...

When I have to choose between my way and God's way, what is the "tipping point" (the reason for my decision) for me when I choose between one and the other?

When is the last time I've experienced the Lord's green pastures and quiet waters?

What practical things do I need to do in order to make green pastures and quiet waters a normal part of my Christian life?

Prayer:

Lord Jesus, I so want your way and not mine. Pour out Your grace upon me and help me to lie down in Your green pastures of blessing. Pour out Your grace upon me and lead me beside those still, peaceful waters where I feel safe and secure in Your love.

Psalms of Discipleship—Principle #44

Life Principles For Those Who Choose To Follow Jesus And Live The Discipled Life

Key Scripture: He restores my soul; He guides me in the paths of righteousness For His name's sake. **Psalm 23:3**

Core Value: Grace

The term "dead men walking" can describe the person who is only a shell of themselves; existing, surviving, but hardly experiencing a full and vibrant life. Anyone who has walked with the Lord for any amount of time can testify that life can be hard, challenging, and at times, down right exhausting. One's soul does become battered, damaged, and severely fatigued. And that is what happens on "good" days. Fortunately, there is One who not only "gets" what we are going through, He desires to help. What we cannot do (restoration of the soul), the Shepherd does. This is called grace. Cloud and Townsend offer their helpful perspective on the human need for grace and for the need to be heard (by those in our community and by God):

"To grow, we need things that we do not have and cannot provide, and we need to have a source of those things who looks favorably upon us and who does things for us for our own good." Pg. 67

"As Hebrews 4:16 says, 'Let us then approach the throne of grace with confidence, so that we may receive mercy and find grace to help us in our time of need.' Grace teaches us that God is inclined to help us in our failure and that he sees our inability as part of reality and he is not mad at our weakness. In fact, he calls it a 'blessed' state, our being unable to do what we need to do (Matt. 5:3; 2 Cor. 12:9-10)." Pg. 69

"Jesus knows about our suffering through his own experience . . . Jesus put himself in a unique position by his suffering. If anyone can say about our situation, 'I've been there,' it is he." Pg. 90

"One of the most important aspects to growth in our suffering is that we need to know that we are understood. This is what provides empathy for us. We cannot grow if we are all alone emotionally. Life is too difficult. But if we know that someone truly understands, we know that we are not alone with our feelings and thoughts, and we gain encouragement to persevere in our growth. We need to know that we are 'heard'—on a human level from each other, and on a divine level from God . . ." Pg. 92

Cloud, Henry and Townsend, John. 2001. *How people grow: what the Bible reveals about personal growth*. Grand Rapids, MI: Zondervan.

Experiencing soul fatigue? The Lord will restore your soul.

Principle #44 & Personal Application: Quality disciples have an on-going testimony of receiving divine restoration and perfect guidance.

- It is only the grace of God that can *restore* the human soul. How does He restore us? He, and only He, can repair, restore, and redeem a damaged soul by His awesome healing power.
- It is only the grace of God that can *guide* the disciple of Jesus Christ in the paths of righteousness. How does He guide us? He does it like a Shepherd, a Good Shepherd who leads, guides, protects, provides, comforts and makes a way for us on the righteous paths of life.
- It is only the grace of God that *blesses* us and gives Him the glory—all of it. Why does He bless us? He does it for His name's sake. It gives the Lord great joy to reveal His name to us as Jehovah Shalom—the Lord is our Peace; as El Shaddai, the All Sufficient One; as Jehovah Rapha, the Lord our Healer.

Reflect & Respond: Some Really Good Questions To Ponder...

What is it that has damaged my soul? What do I need (i.e., healing, renewal, encouragement) the Lord to do that will restore my soul?

As I read my Bible, where in God's Word has He been speaking to me and what has He been saying that is giving me the Lord's guidance of my life?

In the Bible, there are many names given to God. Which ones have been the most meaningful to me this past month?

Prayer:
 Lord Jesus, You and only You can restore my soul. I have been wounded by sin and need Your healing touch in my life. May I always be teachable so that when I am guided by You, I will find myself on paths of righteousness for Your name's sake.

Psalms of Discipleship—Principle #45

Life Principles For Those Who Choose To Follow Jesus And Live The Discipled Life

Key Scripture: Even though I walk through the valley of the shadow of death, I fear no evil, for You are with me; Your rod and Your staff, they comfort me. **Psalm 23:4**

Core Value: Grace

What is it that really scares us? Is it being misunderstood or being isolated and alone? Does the thought of failing health cause us to fear? Or does the worry of not having enough money set aside to take care of present and future needs cause us to panic? Does the fear of the unknown paralyze us from making any plans for the future? When confronted with a somewhat ominous journey through the valley of the shadow of death, what is the disciple of Jesus to do? When the dark clouds seem to overwhelm us, we must walk in faith. In his book, *The shape of faith to come: spiritual formation and the future of discipleship*, Brad Waggoner writes about the kind of faith that is needed for the disciple:

"Faith is often confused with a general sense of optimism or a vague sense that things will work out in the end. But this is not equivalent to biblical faith, which is rooted in the conviction that God is in full control of all things and that He has a purpose in every situation." Pg. 183

"Exercising faith requires that we run in such a way that we win—that is, win in doing the will of God and running with a faith that abandons any option but God's." Pg. 188

God is in control . . . and we are not. Walking in His perfect will is always our best choice. These two gifts (grace and faith) from the Lord allow us walk through any challenges that come our way with His joy, His comfort, and His peace.

Principle #45 & Personal Application: Quality disciples have the most incredible sense of God's comfort and care.

- We have been given great grace that *sustains* us in the most challenging of times. Everyone, sometime, will have to walk through the valley of the shadow of death.
- We have been given great grace that *comforts* us when horrible fear abounds. Everyone, sometime, if we have faith, will experience a marvelous sense of peace even when evil seeks to overwhelm and conquer the disciple.

Reflect & Respond: Some Really Good Questions To Ponder…

What kinds of feelings do I experience when I go through my own valley of the shadow of death?

How has God's rod and staff been a comfort to me?

Prayer:

Lord Jesus, I am so grateful for your great grace that richly abounds in my life when I am going through the valley of the shadow of death. I am comforted knowing that evil, though powerful and foreboding at times, cannot steal my peace. I feel safe as I sense the care of Your protection. In spite of my own harried circumstances, I am comforted by Your rod and staff. May I always look to You as the Good Shepherd who gives a grace that is sustaining and comforting.

Psalms of Discipleship—Principle #46

Life Principles For Those Who Choose To Follow Jesus And Live The Discipled Life

Key Scripture: You prepare a table before me in the presence of my enemies; You have anointed my head with oil; My cup overflows. **Psalm 23:5**

Core Value: Grace

Wouldn't it be nice if just being a "good" Christian meant having a life of ease and pleasure? Wouldn't it be great if everyone got along and there would be no conflict? Wouldn't it be . . . completely unrealistic? The message of the Cross declares a completely different view of life. By definition, the Cross is a symbol of suffering and death. We are told to take up our cross, deny our self and follow Jesus. One of the beautiful truths from the Scriptures are the promises made to the believer who is undergoing difficult circumstances. In the midst of our trouble, the Lord is with us in a very special way. It all begins with having a personal, growing relationship with Jesus Christ. Michael Wilkins offers this perspective:

"When Jesus called men and women to follow him, he offered a personal relationship with himself, not simply an alternative lifestyle or different religious practices or a new social organization . . . Discipleship means the beginning of a new life in intimate fellowship with a living Master and Savior." Pg. 355

Wilkins, Michael J. 1992. *Following the Master: discipleship in the steps of Jesus.* Grand Rapids, MI: Zondervan Publishing House.

The grace of God (having an intimate fellowship with Lord) allows us not only to *survive,* but also *thrive* in the midst of extraordinary circumstances.

Principle #46 & Personal Application: Quality disciples are the recipients of the most extraordinary *care* in the most extraordinary of *circumstances.*

- The grace of God is given to the disciple of Jesus Christ, no matter how difficult the circumstances appear to be.
- The grace of God is given to the disciple of Jesus Christ, poured out upon us as He anoints us with His grace.

- The grace of God is given to the disciple of Jesus Christ, with an abundance that overflows our life.

Reflect & Respond: Some Really Good Questions To Ponder...

Can I recall a time when Jesus "prepared a table before me in the presence of my enemies?" What did I learn about His faithfulness to me?

Am I experiencing an overflow life of grace where my cup is overflowing? What is the secret to having a life where one's cup does overflow . . . continually?

Prayer:

Lord Jesus, You are well aware of the spiritual battles I am fighting today. The battle is intense and at times (sometimes) I want to give up and give in to the enemy of my soul. Yet, Your great promise to me is that You will prepare a table before me in the presence of my enemies. You will anoint my head with oil. You will see that my cup will not be able to contain itself, but will overflow with your blessed grace. Lord may I be drenched with Your grace as I sit in peace at this table You are preparing before me.

The Essential Core Values Of The Quality Disciple Are...
Grace—Worship—Bible Study—Prayer—Community—Service—Evangelism

Psalms of Discipleship—Principle #47

Life Principles For Those Who Choose To Follow Jesus And Live The Discipled Life

Key Scripture: Surely goodness and lovingkindness will follow me all the days of my life, And I will dwell in the house of the LORD forever. **Psalm 23:6**

Core Value: Grace

Life is uncertain. There are certain times in the disciple's journey that times of transition and change can be down right scary. Try as we might to appear to be in control, in reality, we are not. When we sense we are losing our grip on control, fear is not far behind as it seeks to invade our heart. We race ahead, seeking to outrace our rapidly beating heart. Sometimes, during the course of our journey, we run to a place where fear rules: the cliffs of uncertainty that drain into the pit of unbelief. God knows of this place too (Psalm 139:7-12). It is where He seeks to meet us with His "posse" of goodness and lovingkindness that are continually at work to round us up and lead us to an eternal life with Him. In his book, *Choose the Life*, Bill Hull suggests:

> "There is a myth afoot that says as I grow spiritually I become less needy and less dependent, and after a certain discipleship regime I will have it together. Discipleship is a lifelong process, and I will be extremely needy until that wonderful moment I am completely and eternally changed. In fact the more I become like Jesus, the more I am dependent on him." Pg. 180

We who follow Jesus will always be in need of His goodness and lovingkindness. And when they have completed their task with us, we will be at home, forever in His presence.

Principle #47 & Personal Application: Quality disciples cannot escape from the pursuit of God's goodness and lovingkindness as they shadow him or her all the way to the house of the Lord.

What kind of grace is it that one cannot escape?

- The kind of grace that sends out in pursuit goodness and lovingkindness for the disciple of Jesus Christ.
- The kind of grace that never stops pursuing us every day of our lives.
- The kind of grace that will be our heavenly escort as we are ushered into and dwell in the house of the Lord forever.

Reflect & Respond: Some Really Good Questions To Ponder...

What kinds of feelings well up in my heart when I ponder God's goodness and lovingkindness in my life?

Have I ever contemplated what it is going to be like when the Lord calls me home to live with Him forever?

Prayer:

Lord Jesus, my faith is sure in knowing that You have sent goodness and lovingkindness after me, to pursue me, to shadow me, to escort me as I walk with You in this life. And when my life on this earth is over and done, I will come into Your glorious presence and live in Your house forever. May my heart always rejoice in Your grace. Because the Lord is my Shepherd, I have everything that I need—both now and into eternity.

The Essential Core Values Of The Quality Disciple Are...
Grace—Worship—Bible Study—Prayer—Community—Service—Evangelism

Psalms of Discipleship—Principle #48

Life Principles For Those Who Choose To Follow Jesus And Live The Discipled Life

Key Scripture: [4] Make me know Your ways, O LORD; Teach me Your paths. [5] Lead me in Your truth and teach me, For You are the God of my salvation; For You I wait all the day. **Psalm 24:4-5**

Core Value: Bible Study

As disciples of Jesus Christ we do not have to be left guessing of what His will is for our life. The Psalmist has turned this need into a prayer of knowledge; but not knowledge only, but also a passionate request for a deeper relationship with God. Many a believer has misplaced the use of the Scriptures to one's spiritual growth. Yes, we must be devoted students of God's Word and read it and personally apply it. But, we must desire above all a growing relationship with the God of the Bible. Scot McKnight underscores this when he writes,

> What is my relationship to the *God* of the Bible? Our relationship is not so much with the Bible but with the *God* of the Bible. There's a difference that makes a big difference. Pg. 84

> There is more to the Bible than its subject matter. In fact, the dynamic involved is earth-shattering and ought to revolutionize how we approach the Bible. It is . . . the *relational approach*. So, let me build a relational approach to the Bible, one that finds resonance with the delightful obedience of the psalmist, one that sees God's words as personal words . . . The relational approach turns the Bible from facts-only to facts-that-lead-to-engagement with the God of the Bible. Pg. 87

> McKnight, Scot. 2008. *The blue parakeet: rethinking how you read the Bible.* Grand Rapids, MI: Zondervan.

May we all desire to know The Lord more and more, each and every day.

Principle #48 & Personal Application: Quality disciples are teachable and know the true story of Christmas is found in the Bible.

- It is because of the story of Christmas (the birth of Christ) that we can know His ways. Jesus came to reveal God to us. This is called the incarnation.
- It is because of the story of Christmas (the birth of Christ) that we can learn His paths. Jesus came to give us direction that will lead to spending eternity with Him. This is called the narrow way.
- It is because of the story of Christmas (the birth of Christ) that we can be led in His truth and be taught. Jesus came to reveal truth to us. This is called His Word.
- It is because of the story of Christmas (the birth of Christ) that we can have a relationship with the God of our salvation. Jesus was well worth the wait!

Reflect & Respond: Some Really Good Questions To Ponder…

What commitments do I need to make in order to keep my focus on Jesus this Christmas?

Jesus is the God of my salvation. How will this fact impact my life during the Christmas season?

Prayer:

Lord Jesus, as I contemplate the Advent of Your first coming, please keep reminding me of why You came. May I know Your ways; may I learn Your paths; may I be led in Your truth and may I rejoice in a fresh expression of worship of You as the God of my salvation.

Psalms of Discipleship—Principle #49

Life Principles For Those Who Choose To Follow Jesus And Live The Discipled Life

Key Scripture: Do not remember the sins of my youth or my transgressions; According to Your lovingkindness remember me, For Your goodness' sake, O LORD. **Psalm 25:7**

Core Value: Grace

Somewhere along the way, many of those who claim to be followers of Jesus, have been poisoned by the false belief that God demands perfection from us. *"If we really love Him, we will not sin."* Theologically, we might push back on that statement. But what we really believe in our core and how we live out the Christian journey will ultimately tell the truth about us. We can become more spiritual than God, refusing to forgive ourselves, when God has already done so. Dallas Willard reminds us that a life of grace is not defined by how many right answers about the Bible we possess.

"The narrow gate is not, as so often assumed, doctrinal correctness. The narrow gate is obedience—and the confidence in Jesus necessary to it. We can see that it is not doctrinal correctness because many people who cannot even understand the correct doctrines nevertheless place their full faith in him. Moreover, we find many people who seem to be very correct doctrinally but have hearts full of hatred and unforgiveness." Pg. 275

"So life in the kingdom is not just a matter of *not* doing what is wrong. The apprentices of Jesus are primarily occupied with the positive good that can be done during their days 'under the sun' and the positive strengths and virtues that they develop in themselves as they grow toward 'the kingdom prepared for them from the foundations of the world' (Matt. 25:34)." Pg. 284-285

Willard, Dallas. 1998. *The Divine Conspiracy: Rediscovering Our Hidden Life in God.* San Francisco, CA: HarperSanFrancisco.

Because He loves us and has forgiven us through His work on the Cross, we can forgive ourselves too.

Principle #49 & Personal Application: Quality disciples celebrate the incredible gift of forgiveness—past, present and future.

We were given an incredible gift of grace . . .

- When Jesus Christ forgave the sins in our past, present, and future. [Do not remember the sins of my youth or my transgressions]
- When we were shown the lovingkindness of the Lord. [According to Your lovingkindness remember me]
- When our feeble prayers were directed to a good God. [For Your goodness' sake, O LORD]
- When God became flesh (the incarnation) and entered our neighborhood. Immanuel, God with us.

Reflect & Respond: Some Really Good Questions To Ponder…

Is there anything I have done in my past where I have not forgiven myself? What is the secret to experiencing God's forgiveness of my sin?

There are some who may view God as an unforgiving tyrant who is just waiting to punish us for our sin. Do I see God as a loving heavenly Father who wants to set me free from my guilt and shame?

Prayer:

Lord Jesus, it is because of Your grace and Your grace alone that I can approach You and plead my case. Lord, I beseech You: please do not remember the sins of my youth or my many transgressions. Lord, according to Your lovingkindess remember me for Your goodness' sake.

Psalms of Discipleship—Principle #50

Life Principles For Those Who Choose To Follow Jesus And Live The Discipled Life

Key Scripture: Who is the man who fears the LORD? He will instruct him in the way he should choose. **Psalm 25:12**

Core Value: Prayer

"What should I do?" "Where should I go?" "Who should I marry?" "How will I know what to do and when to do it?" These are examples of the kinds of questions a disciple of Jesus may wrestle with on life's journey of faith. All good questions, for sure. Here is the good news: the pressure is off! We do not have to resolve these kinds of questions on our own. Listen carefully to the counsel of the Psalmist: "Who is the man who fears the LORD? He will instruct him in the way he should choose." Receiving supernatural direction for life is simply a matter of cause and effect: If we fear the Lord (give Him reverence, respect, hold Him in awe), then He will instruct us in the way we should choose. Note: He will not turn us into mindless robots. We still must make a choice to obey and walk it out in faith.

It is through the means of prayer we discover that "answered" prayer is more than getting what we want from God. Prayer is only a means to an end; that we might get to know the Lord better as we dialogue with Him. Getting direction from Him is best accomplished when we have a growing relationship with Him. Richard Foster adds this important contribution to the importance of relationship when he writes,

> "Slowly, almost imperceptibly, there is a shift in our center of gravity. We pass thinking of God as part of our life to the realization that we are part of His life." (Pg. 15) Foster, Richard. 1992. P*rayer: Finding the Heart's True Home*. San Francisco, CA: HarperSanFrancisco.

May each one of us who are disciples of Jesus come to a fresh realization that we are an important part of God's life. He wants to have a relationship with His children. Because of His desire and our need for relationship, may we take every life choice we face before His Throne of Grace (Hebrews 4:16)

Principle #50 & Personal Application: Quality disciples cultivate a disciplined habit: every life choice that is made is bathed in prayer.

When we fear (greatly respect and honor) the Lord . . .

- It will have a significant impact on how we pray.
- We will be so close to hearing His heart that we are willing to seek His will, and not our own.
- We will have a blessed assurance that the path we choose will be the correct decision.
- We gain a fresh perspective of why God sent His Son to our world: to provide a way for us to experience eternal life. This is the wonderful story of Christmas. God made a choice...so must we.

Reflect & Respond: Some Really Good Questions To Ponder...

What does my life look like as a disciple of Jesus Christ? Do I live my life in fear of the Lord; do I greatly respect and honor Him?

How do I know for sure that the life choices I make are at the center of God's will for me?

Prayer:

Lord Jesus, teach me how to fear God in the right way. Teach me how to respect and honor You. May my life be marked by a life of prayer that governs the choices I make. May I never seek my way as a replacement for Your way. May I be the kind of disciple who knows Your heart so well that I instinctively follow Your instruction on the way I should choose.

Psalms of Discipleship—Principle #51

Life Principles For Those Who Choose To Follow Jesus And Live The Discipled Life

Key Scripture: Examine me, O LORD, and try me; Test my mind and my heart. **Psalm 26:2**

Core Value: Prayer

"Are you honest with God?" This is the question that cuts through any kind of "religious" spirit and goes to the heart of what is true or what is just a spiritual mirage. The prayer of the Psalmist was one of honesty and a pure desire to become "real" with God. Note the clear directions the Psalmist gave to the Lord: "Examine me . . . try me . . . test my mind . . . and my heart." No holding back here in an attempt to be seen as something he was not. In essence, the Psalmist was asking God for restoration, a fresh and healthy relationship with his God. It is tempting to ignore what we need from God: to give Him permission to inspect our mind and heart. Over time, we may drift and adapt and live life without God's supernatural redemptive power. In the book, "The Rest of God" by Mark Buchanan, he offers a unique perspective on how challenging it is to open one's life to God's review.

> "A curious thing about restoration is that it doesn't need doing. Strictly speaking, life carries on without it. Restoration is an invasion of sorts. It's fixing something that's broken, but broken so long it's almost mended . . . Restoration meddles with what [we've] learned to handle, removes what [we've] learned to live with, bestows what [we've] learned to live without. Replacements have been found already, thank you all the same." Pg. 150

May we never become satisfied with the "status quo." May the Lord give us the grace we need to prayerfully ask Him to inspect us, from the inside out.

Principle #51 & Personal Application: Quality disciples invite an honest and transparent assessment of what one thinks and feels inside.

It is by prayer that the disciple of Jesus Christ:

- Can become "real" with God. "Examine me, O Lord." This coming year I can be honest to God.

- Can welcome an honest assessment from the Lord. "Try me." This coming year I can be willing to take the risk that God knows what is best for me.

- Can trust the Lord's probing of what is at one's inner core. "Test my mind and my heart." This coming year I can peel away the onion of my life and see what is most important to me.

- Can embrace the One who came into the world as a baby but is now our risen Savior. "Christ in us, the hope of glory." This coming year I can renew my commitment to live my life for Him.

Reflect & Respond: Some Really Good Questions To Ponder...

Do I find it easy or challenging to be real with God? Why?

What kinds of things do I conceal in my mind and heart that are not in alignment with God's Word?

Prayer:
  Lord Jesus, I give You permission to check me out—on the inside. Please examine me, O Lord. Please try me and test my mind and heart...and then, Lord, please overwhelm me with Your grace as You form my mind into the mind of Christ; as You create in me a clean heart; as You once again, renew my focus to live for You.

Psalms of Discipleship—Principle #52

Life Principles For Those Who Choose To Follow Jesus And Live The Discipled Life

Key Scripture: [7] Hear, O LORD, when I cry with my voice, And be gracious to me and answer me. [8] *When You said,* "Seek My face," my heart said to You, "Your face, O LORD, I shall seek." [9] Do not hide Your face from me, Do not turn Your servant away in anger; You have been my help; Do not abandon me nor forsake me, O God of my salvation! **Psalm 27:7-9**

Core Value: Prayer

The gift of prayer is a wonderful resource . . . if the disciple of Jesus is willing to use it. We know it is there. We know of its benefit to the believer. And we know prayer is what our Lord desires us to do, on a frequent basis. And yet, for many of us, we find it difficult, seeming nearly impossible, to develop a healthy habit of meaningful prayer. Why is this? Perhaps, it is due to what Donald Whitney describes as "an impersonal requirement":

"Don't think of prayer as an impersonal requirement. Realize that it is a Person, the Lord Jesus Christ, with all authority and with all love, who expects us to pray." (Pg. 67) Whitney, Donald S. 1991. *Spiritual disciplines for the Christian life*. Colorado Springs, CO: NavPress.

Has prayer become another religious "duty" that we simply check off of our so-called spirituality list and then move on to more of the same: an empty and unfulfilling relationship with the Lord? There are many things that we can do on our own that will give the illusion that we are something that we are not. A life marked by the power of prayer, biblical prayer, is not one of them. By God's grace, may He renew our focus upon the One who desires to have an ongoing, intimate relationship with us.

The Psalmist has a lot to say about the intimacy and necessity of prayer. He reminds us that the God of the Universe desires to hear the voice of His child. He desires to answer prayers that are offered according to His perfect will. He has promised to walk with us, no matter how challenging are our circumstances. Our responsibility is to keep our eyes fixed upon Jesus, the Founder and Perfecter of our faith (Hebrews 12:2) and talk to and listen to Him.

Principle #52 & Personal Application: Quality disciples have a laser-like focus to keep the face of the Lord in clear view.

When I seek the Lord, face to face:

- I am reminded of His desire to hear my voice.
- I am reminded of His desire to answer me.
- I am reminded of His desire to be kind to me and not to turn away from me in anger.
- I am reminded of His desire not to abandon or forsake me but to comfort me with His presence.
- I am reminded of His desire to be the God of my salvation!

Reflect & Respond: Some Really Good Questions To Ponder...

What kinds of things do I need to do for the following year that will help me keep my focus upon the Lord?

When I make an effort to seek the face of the Lord, what kind of impact does it make upon my life?

Prayer:
Lord Jesus, may this coming year be one of a renewed intimacy with You. May prayer not become a trite thing that I do, but a transforming way of life. When I seek Your face, may You impress upon my heart the beauty of Your face.

TOPICAL INDEX (Means of Growth for the Quality Disciple)

Topic	Psalm	Personal Application	Page
Grace			
	3:3	Quality disciples deeply acknowledge and appreciate the gracious care of the Lord.	23
	4:3	Quality disciples personally experience God's grace.	29
	5:11-12	Quality disciples, deeply moved by the grace of God, experience unbridled joy that results in adoration and praise.	37
	9:9-10	Quality disciples have the confident assurance that there is a safe place in Him.	49
	13:5-6	Quality disciples respond to the grace of God with trust, rejoicing, and singing.	59
	16:5-6	Quality disciples are *so* blessed because of God's grace.	63
	16:11	Quality disciples experience a fulfilled life marked by the grace of God.	67
	17:8	Quality disciples take great delight in being one of God's prized possessions.	71
	18:35-36	Quality disciples are sobered by God's all-consuming grace.	79
	23:1	Quality disciples lack for nothing because the Lord has provided everything that is needed.	99
	23:2	Quality disciples experience the blessing of abundant provision and restful peace when they submit their will to God.	101
	23:3	Quality disciples have an on-going testimony of receiving divine restoration and perfect guidance.	103

Topic	Psalm	Personal Application	Page
	23:4	Quality disciples have the most incredible sense of God's comfort and care.	105
	23:5	Quality disciples are the recipients of the most extraordinary *care* in the most extraordinary of *circumstances*.	107
	23:6	Quality disciples cannot escape from the pursuit of God's goodness and lovingkindness as they shadow him or her all the way to the house of the Lord.	109
	25:7	Quality disciples celebrate the incredible gift of forgiveness—past, present and future.	113

Topic	Psalm	Personal Application	Page
Worship			
	2:11	Quality disciples choose a way of life that is driven by a passionate worship of God expressing itself in humble service to Him.	21
	5:7	Quality disciples have a keen and reverent respect for the Lord and hearts that seek to worship God.	33
	5:11-12	Quality disciples, deeply moved by the grace of God, experience unbridled joy that results in adoration and praise.	35
	7:17	Quality disciples practice a worship that is centered upon the character and majesty of God.	41
	8:1	Quality disciples are overwhelmed with awe and wonder of who God is.	43
	9:1-2	Quality disciples practice an active and vibrant worship of God.	47

Topic	Psalm	Personal Application	Page
	11:7	Quality disciples have a high and exalted view of Almighty God.	53
	16:7-8	Quality disciples, with a heart of worship, have a laser-like focus upon the Lord.	65
	18:1-3	Quality disciples offer a dynamic worship of the Lord from a heart that knows Him personally: He is mine!	73
	18:46	Quality disciples have a keen awareness of the greatness of God.	81
	19:1	Quality disciples are struck by the wonder of God's marvelous creation.	83
	19:14	Quality disciples experience an authentic worship that is both verbal and non-verbal.	87
	20:7	Quality disciples do not worship anything or anyone other than Jesus Christ.	91
	21:13	Quality disciples have a heart to worship the One who is exalted and worthy of praise.	95

Topic	Psalm	Personal Application	Page
Bible Study			
	1:2-3	Quality disciples place great value in spending quality time in God's Word.	19
	12:6	Quality disciples have a high regard for the Word of God.	55
	18:30	Quality disciples find great comfort and joy in the Word of God.	77

Topic	Psalm	Personal Application	Page
	19:7-11	Quality disciples have an unquenchable passion to *know* and *experience* the Word of God.	85
	24:4-5	Quality disciples are teachable and know the true story of Christmas is found in the Bible.	111

Topic	Psalm	Personal Application	Page
Prayer			
	3:4	Quality disciples experience an intimate and interactive dialogue with God in prayer.	25
	4:1	Quality disciples fully expect God to answer prayer.	27
	4:3	Quality disciples personally experience God's grace.	29
	5:1-3	Quality disciples have dynamic lives, marked by the spiritual discipline of prayer and a firm expectation that God is at work.	31
	6:9	Quality disciples not only *pray* to the Lord, but also know that God *hears*.	37
	7:1	Quality disciples know that prayer offered in Jesus' name will lead them to put trust in the One who is their Refuge.	39
	10:17	Quality disciples know the Lord—are intimately acquainted with Jesus—and are known by Him.	51
	13:1-4	Quality disciples will pray, even though the circumstances of life are crushing.	57

Topic	Psalm	Personal Application	Page
	17:6	Quality disciples cry out in prayer to a God who will not only *listen* but also *answer*.	69
	18:6	Quality disciples do not hesitate to cry out to God for help.	75
	20:1	Quality disciples fully expect God to answer prayer His way and in His time in the crucible of crisis.	89
	20:9	Quality disciples long to experience the power of corporate prayer.	93
	25:12	Quality disciples cultivate a disciplined habit: every life choice that is made is bathed in prayer.	115
	26:2	Quality disciples invite an honest and transparent assessment of what one thinks and feels inside.	117
	27:7-9	Quality disciples have a laser-like focus to keep the face of the Lord in clear view.	119

Topic	Psalm	Personal Application	Page
Community	1:1	Quality disciples place great value in being a part of a biblical community with other disciples of Christ.	17
	15:1-5	Quality disciples treat others with great respect.	61
	20:9	Quality disciples long to experience the power of corporate prayer.	93

Topic	Psalm	Personal Application	Page
Service			
	2:11	Quality disciples choose a way of life that is driven by a passionate worship of God expressing itself in humble service to Him.	21
	8:4-6	Quality disciples are responsible and devoted managers of God's assets.	45

Topic	Psalm	Personal Application	Page
Evangelism			
	22:27	Quality disciples have a heart for the Lord of the Harvest.	97

Topical Bibliography for the Quality Disciple

Spiritual Disciplines

1. Foster, Richard. 1988. *Celebration of discipline: the path to spiritual growth.* San Francisco, CA: Harper San Francisco.
2. Willard, Dallas. 1988. *The spirit of the disciplines: understanding how God changes lives.* San Francisco, CA: Harper San Francisco.

Prayer

3. Foster, Richard. 1992. P*rayer: Finding the Heart's True Home.* San Francisco, CA: Harper San Francisco.
4. Lockyer, Herbert. 1959. *All the prayers of the Bible.* Grand Rapids, MI: Zondervan.
5. Murray, Andrew. 1983, reprint. *Living a prayerful life.* Minneapolis, MN: Bethany House.
6. Duewel, Wesley L. 1986. *Touch the world through prayer.* Grand Rapids, MI: Francis Asbury Press.
7. Bounds, E. M. 2004. *The complete works of E. M. Bounds on prayer.* Grand Rapids, MI: Baker Books.
8. Sanders, J. Oswald. 1980. *Spiritual leadership.* Chicago, IL: Moody Press.

Bible Study

9. McKnight, Scot. 2008. *The blue parakeet: rethinking how you read the Bible.* Grand Rapids, MI: Zondervan.
10. McQuilkin, Robertson. 1992. *Understanding and applying the Bible,* Chicago, IL: Moody Press.
11. Peterson, Eugene H. 2006. *Eat this book: a conversation in the art of spiritual reading.* Grand Rapids, MI: Wm. B. Eerdmans Publishing Co.

Worship

12. MacDonald, James. 2006. *Downpour.* Nashville, TN: Broadman & Holdman.
13. Thomas, Gary. 2000. *Sacred Pathways: discover your soul's path to God, first Zondervan edition.* Grand Rapids, MI: Zondervan.

Grace

14. Strombeck, J. F. 1947, (2nd edition). *Disciplined by grace: studies in Christian conduct.* Moline, IL. Strombeck Agency, Inc; distributed by Van Kampen Press, Chicago, IL.
15. Swindoll, Charles, R. 2003. *The Grace Awakening.* Nashville, TN: W Publishing Group.

Community
16. Bates, Denny. 2005. *Building a Christian community of friends.* Florence, SC: Something New Christian Publishers.
17. Crabb, Larry. 1999. *The safest place on earth: where people connect and are forever changed.* Nashville, TN: Word Publishing.

Service
18. Rees, Erik. 2006. *S.H.A.P.E.: finding and fulfilling your unique purpose for life.* Grand Rapids, MI: Zondervan.

Evangelism
19. Coleman, Robert E. 1963, 1964, 1993. [New Spire edition 1994]. *The master plan of evangelism.* Grand Rapids, MI: Fleming H. Revell.
20. McQuilkin, Robertson. 1984, 2002 (rev). *The great omission.* Waynesboro, GA: Authentic Media.
21. Pippert, Rebecca Manley. 1979. *Out of the salt shaker and into the world.* Downers Grove, IL: InterVarsity Press.

Discipleship and the Christian Life
22. Allender, Dan B. 2006. *Leading with a limp: turning your struggles into strengths.* Colorado Springs, CO: Waterbrook Press.
23. Anderson, Keith R. and Reese, Randy D. 1999. *Spiritual mentoring: a guide for seeking and giving direction.* Downers Grove, IL: InterVarsity Press.
24. Arn, Win and Charles. 1998. *The master's plan for making disciples, 2nd edition.* Grand Rapids, MI: Baker Books.
25. Barna, George. 2001. *Growing true disciples: new strategies for producing genuine followers of Christ.* Colorado Springs, CO: Waterbrook Press.
26. Biehl, Bobb. 1996. *Mentoring: confidence in finding a mentor and becoming one.* Nashville, TN: Broadman and Holman Publishers.
27. Blackaby, Henry and Richard. 2001. *Spiritual leadership: moving people to God's agenda.* Nashville, TN: Broadman & Holman Publishers.
28. Boa, Kenneth. 2006. *The perfect leader: practicing the leadership traits of God.* Colorado Springs, CO: Victor (Cook Communications Ministries).
29. Burchett, Harold E. 1980. *Spiritual Life Studies.* Published by the author.
30. Campbell, James R. 2009. *Mentor like Jesus.* Nashville, TN: B & H Publishing Group.
31. Chambers, Oswald. 1985. *Christian disciplines: volumes 1 and 2.* Grand Rapids, MI: Chosen Books.
32. Chan, Simon. 1998. *Spiritual theology: a systematic theology of the Christian life.* Downers Grove, IL: InterVarsity Press.

33. Clinton, J. Robert and Richard W. 1991. *The mentor handbook.* Altadena, CA: Barnabas Publishers.
34. Cloud, Henry and Townsend, John. 2001. *How people grow: what the Bible reveals about personal growth.* Grand Rapids, MI: Zondervan.
35. Coleman, Robert E. 1987. *The Master Plan of Discipleship.* Old Tappan, NJ: Fleming H. Revell.
36. Hagberg, Janet O., and Guelich, Robert A. 2005, 1995. *The critical journey: stages in the life of faith.* Salem, WI: Sheffield Publishing Company.
37. Hanks, Billie Jr., and Shell, William A. 1982. *Discipleship: the best writings from the most experienced disciplemakers.* Grand Rapids, MI: The Zondervan Corporation.
38. Harney, Kevin. 2007. *Leadership from the inside out: examining the inner life of a healthy church leader.* Grand Rapids, MI: Zondervan.
39. Hart, Arcihbald D. 1995. *Adrenaline and Stress.* Nashville, TN: W. Publishing Group.
40. Hawkins, Greg L., Parkinson, Cally, and Arnson, Eric. 2007. *Reveal.* Barrington, IL: Willow Creek Resources.
41. Hawkins, Greg L. and Parkinson, Cally. 2008. *Follow me.* Barrington, IL: Willow Creek Resources.
42. Hendricks, Howard and William. 1995. *As iron sharpens iron.* Chicago, IL: Moody Publishers.
43. Hettinga, Jan David. 1996. *Follow me: experience the loving leadership of Jesus.* Colorado Springs, CO: NavPress.
44. Hull, Bill. 2004. *Choose the life: exploring a faith that embraces discipleship.* Grand Rapids, MI: Baker Books.
45. Hull, Bill. 1990. *The disciple-making church.* Grand Rapids, MI: Fleming H. Revell.
46. Hull, Bill. 1995. *Building high commitment in a low commitment world.* Grand Rapids, MI: Fleming H. Revell.
47. Hull, Robert W. 2006. *The complete book of discipleship.* Colorado Springs. NavPress.
48. Ingram, Chip. 2007. *Good to great in God's eyes: 10 practices great Christians have in common.* Grand Rapids, MI: Baker Books.
49. Lovelace, Richard J. 1985. *Renewal as a way of life: a guidebook for spiritual growth.* Downers Grove, IL: InterVarsity Press.
50. MacArthur, John F. Jr. 1976. *Keys to spiritual growth.* Old Tappan, NJ: Fleming H. Revell Company.
51. Mancini, Will. 2008. *Church unique: how missional leaders cast vision, capture culture, and create movement.* San Francisco, CA: Jossey-Bass.
52. Maxwell, John C. 2005. *The 360-degree leader: developing your influence from anywhere in the organization.* Nashville, TN: Thomas Nelson, Inc.

53. McCallum, Dennis and Lowery, Jessica. 2006. *Organic disciplemaking: mentoring others into spiritual maturity and leadership*. Houston, TX: Touch Publications.

54. McIntosh, Gary L. and Rima, Samuel D., Sr. 1997. *Overcoming the dark side of leadership: the paradox of personal dysfunction*. Grand Rapids, MI: Baker Books.

55. Morley, Patrick, David Delk, and Brett Clemmer. 2006. *No man left behind: how to build a thriving disciple-making ministry for every man in your church*. Chicago, IL: Moody Publishers.

56. Nouwen, Henri J. M. 1975. *Reaching Out: the three movements of the spiritual life*. Garden City, NY: Doubleday and Company, Inc.

57. Ogden, Greg. 2003. *Transforming discipleship: making disciples a few at a time*. Downers Grove, IL: InterVarsity Press.

58. Olson, David T. 2008. *The American church in crisis*. Grand Rapids, MI: Zondervan.

59. Peterson, Jim. 1993. *Lifestyle discipleship: the challenge of following Jesus in today's world*. Colorado Springs, CO: NavPress.

60. Pue, Carson. 2005. *Mentoring leaders: wisdom for developing character, calling, and competency*. Grand Rapids, MI: Baker Books.

61. Putnam, David. 2008. *Breaking the discipleship code*. Nashville, TN: B&H Publishing Group.

62. Sanders, J. Oswald. (1994). *Spiritual discipleship*. Chicago, IL: Moody Publishers.

63. Scazzero, Peter L. (2003). *The emotionally healthy church: a strategy for discipleship that actually changes lives*. Grand Rapids, MI: Zondervan.

64. Stanford, Miles J. 1982. *The green letters: principles of spiritual growth*. Grand Rapids, MI: Zondervan Publishing House.

65. Stanley, Paul D. and Clinton, Robert J. 1992. *Connecting: the mentoring relationships you need to succeed in life*. Colorado Springs, CO: NavPress.

66. Waggoner, Brad J. 2008. *The shape of faith to come: spiritual formation and the future of discipleship*. Nashville, TN: B&H Publishing Group.

67. Willard, Dallas. 1998. *The divine conspiracy: rediscovering our hidden life in God*. San Francisco, CA: HarperSanFrancisco.

68. Willard, Dallas. 2006. *The great omission: reclaiming Jesus's essential teachings on discipleship*. San Francisco, CA: HarperSanFrancisco.

69. Warren, Rick. 1995. *The purpose-driven church*. Grand Rapids, MI: Zondervan.

70. Warren, Rick. 2002. *The purpose-driven life*. Grand Rapids, MI: Zondervan.

71. Wilkins, Michael J. 1992. *Following the Master: discipleship in the steps of Jesus*. Grand Rapids, MI: Zondervan Publishing House.

Essential Spiritual Growth Resources from
Something New Christian Publishers

Websites and Blogs:

www.dennybates.com is the hub for all of our teaching and coaching resources. Check out our free downloads as well as our store.

www.thequalitydisciple.com links to dennybates.com.

www.qualityleadershipconsultants.com links to dennybates.com.

www.thequalitydisciple.blogspot.com is the teaching blog for Psalms of Discipleship.

www.qualityleadershipconsultants.blogspot.com is the teaching blog dedicated to leadership issues in the marketplace and local church.

www.27essentialrules.blogspot.com is a survey of the New Testament, selecting one principle from each book through the lens of discipleship.

www.facebook.com/denny.bates is my portal to social networking.

You can follow me on Twitter @dennybates

Books:

Other titles from the Quality Discipleship Series:
- ❖ Passing It On…How To Make A *Quality* Disciple (E-Book only)
- ❖ How To Study And Apply The Bible To Your Life (E-Book only)
- ❖ Growing Up…Practical Bible Studies For New And Growing Christians (E-Book only)
- ❖ Building A Christian Community Of Friends (E-Book or printed copy)
- ❖ Living Above The Fray (Kindle or Paperback on Amazon)

Retreat Journals:
- ❖ The Power – Broker's Guide To The Kingdom
- ❖ Four Legacies For A Life Change
- ❖ Three Commitments That Change A Life
- ❖ Growing In Grace: A Fresh Look At Biblical Discipleship
- ❖ Adding Quality To Your Life

Contact us for availability and cost.
www.dennybates.com/resouces

QUALITY LEADERSHIP CONSULTANTS: PERSONAL CONSULTING, COACHING, AND COUNSELING

Our Mission:

To present Quality *Ideas* that will produce Quality *Changes* in Quality *Leaders* and *Organizations*

Introducing Professional Life Coach And Consultant, Dr. Denny Bates

Why is it important for you to have a life coach? There are some who erroneously believe that experience is the best guide. We at Quality Leadership Consultants would disagree with that perspective. We believe that *guided experience* is the best guide! Just think of the time, money, and emotional energy you can save by securing the services of a person who already knows what you are feeling and has a good grasp on how to lead you into a positive experience.

Education:
- ❖ B.S. Political Science / Francis Marion University 1979
- ❖ MDiv in Pastoral Ministry / Columbia Graduate School of Bible and Missions (Columbia International University) 1985
- ❖ DMin in Leadership, specializing in personal growth and organizational health / Columbia International University 2011

Professional Credentials:
- ❖ Ordained Pastor since 1985
- ❖ Founder of Something New Christian Publishers
- ❖ Creator of innovative discipleship ministry called DiscipleMakers4Jesus (DM4J)
- ❖ Founding member of the John Maxwell Certification Program
- ❖ Member of American Association of Christian Counselors
- ❖ Member of International Christian Coaching Association
- ❖ Certified in large and small Group Crisis Intervention (Critical Incident Stress Management system—CISM)

Services Rendered: Each client will have the opportunity to unpack the challenges of life with a seasoned life coach who will assist the client in making the best choices for significant life decisions. Special understanding for how to make quality life decisions will come to the client and life coach after a thorough initial interview, appropriate assessments, and the creation of a tested prescription with practical personal application that will lead to growth. I am seasoned in both the market place and non-profit settings. Having both the practical experience and the academic and professional credentials sets me apart from other coaches. I can offer you Quality

Leadership in these five coaching tracks: Personal Growth, Spiritual Growth, Building Healthy Relationships, Career Counseling / Job Performance and Organizational Health.

Within each track are specific "Growth Opportunities" offered by the life coach. Based upon the unique needs of the client, determination on the best approach to take will be agreed upon by the client and life coach. Experience has shown us that it is best to focus upon the greatest need first and then begin to explore other Growth Opportunities. For example, if the client desires to have a life coach assist in reaching Personal Growth goals, he might wish to spend the greatest amount of time working on life management skills (emotional and physical health, financial stewardship, and time management). Due to the unique situation and need of each client, the amount of time invested for each Growth Opportunity is agreed upon by the client and life coach. The initial meeting is offered at no cost to the client. If an agreement is reached between the client and life coach, fees and the number of sessions will then be discussed during the first meeting.

My Targeted Clients are:

- Market Place Leaders, especially corporate executives, who either own their company or have major influence
- Church leaders, including pastors, officers, ministry leaders, couples in ministry
- Spiritually wounded people who have experienced "toxic faith" and have been emotionally or spiritually hurt by organized religion

My Specialties as a Life Coach are:

Life Transitions . . . .

- In <u>Career Changes</u> (Helping Clients Transition With Calling, Training, Mid-Life Crisis Issues)

- In <u>Organizational Health</u> (Helping Clients Transition With Team Building, Overcoming Organizational Poisons)

- In <u>Marital Changes</u> (Helping Clients Transition Through Separation, Divorce or Spousal Death)

- In <u>Legacy Building</u> (Helping Clients Transition By Finishing Well)

Life Training . . . .

- In <u>Preventing Burnout</u> (Helping Clients Transition By Managing Stress And Taking Proactive Steps for Personal Nourishment)

- In <u>Leadership Development</u> (Helping Clients Transition By Learning the Keys to Personal Leadership, Targeting Future Leaders, And Leading Other Leaders)

- In <u>Building Healthy Relationships</u> (Helping Clients Transition By Learning How To Draw Out In Others The Best Qualities, Creating Environments of Grace, Community Building)

- In <u>Spiritual Growth</u> (Helping Clients Transition By Learning How The Seven Means of Spiritual Growth Lead to an Enriched Life)

- In <u>Spiritual Healing</u> (Helping Clients Who Have Been Wounded by Organized Religion Transition Towards Wholeness)

What Others Are Saying:

Here are a few of the testimonies of people I have had the privilege to coach:

Just wanted to let you know how much our time of coaching and leadership development has meant to me. Every time I am faced with a challenge I try to walk thru the Grace tree of wisdom. You set the example every day of the man of God I want to be. Thank you! **(Corporate Manager of Medical Services)**

[I've learned] to keep the main thing the main thing!! To take care of the people that God puts in front of me everyday. **(Sales Manager of automotive dealership)**

Denny has been my friend, pastor, colleague, mentor and confidant for almost 10 years. During this time, Denny has led me through tough waters, given me wise counsel and taught me practical ways to live out my faith while falling more in love with my Savior. **(Youth Pastor)**

Other than my own father, Denny has been my most trusted friend and spiritual mentor. Denny's discipleship has been truly transforming and helped me to realize the importance of investing in others as he has invested in me. **(Medical Device Consultant)**

I treasure my relationship with Denny because we share a common heart to help people discover all that Christ wants to do in and through them. **(Disciple-Making Missionary to Eastern Europe)**

I have known Denny for many years and have had the privilege to work with him on the same pastoral staff for over 5 years. During that time I have sought Denny's counsel on many issues ranging from personal struggles to theological questions. Denny has always provided me with poignant, gracious and thoughtful counsel. They say that everyone should have a mentor and I am blessed to be able to consider Denny my mentor. He has been an invaluable asset in my life and ministry. **(Clinical Counselor)**

My relationship with Denny has been personal, honest, and Christ-centered. Denny's common sense approach to the issues of life is always soundly based on scriptural principles. I remember discussing with Denny how I felt that I needed to do so much service for the Lord because of all the times I had failed Him. Denny gently said to me, "It's all about grace". I was reminded that there is no 'payback' plan for the Lord. **(Pastor)**

Having a group of peers who candidly discuss the awesome responsibility that each carries as a servant and hearing how God has responded so richly to our needs clearly demonstrates how marvelous is our God, who works in each of our lives to do His will. **(Hospital** *Vice-President in a discipleship group for executives)*

Denny and I have know each other for nearly fifteen years, we bonded shortly after he had his heart attack because of an illness I had years prior – Guillain-Barre Syndrome – that made me more aware of the right priorities I should have in life. Through this episode and having children similar in age we bonded in a unique and special way rarely achieved between men. Approximately one year ago I lost my job as a senior executive at a large international company that I had been with 26 years, during the transition period of me finding another job Denny was an extreme encouragement to me. During a time when I was wrestling between accepting a position or not and I will never forget what Denny told me "You can just accept it as God's providential care". He was right! I later humbly accepted the position as President & Chief Operating Officer for a Subsea Oilfield Manufacturing company. **(Corporate Executive)**

Denny has been a teacher / mentor / discipler / encourager / prayer partner and great friend who God has used to help me keep a godly perspective on the different times & issues of life I've gone through as I've seek to follow Jesus. Once while praying with Denny through a career move, he encouraged me to think of the gifts & skills I had and then ask what I had a passion for, and then to ask God to show me how they can fit together. From this I learned to stop putting these gifts & skills in a "Box" and limiting what God could do with them, and use them for. For the first time, as I now work for a non-profit Christian organization as a warehouse manager, I feel I'm using the gifts and abilities God has given me to fulfill His purpose at something I really have a passion for! **(Former** *market place worker, now Missionary who is impacting the world)*

Denny met with me at 7 a.m. every Friday for a year. He came to me knowing he would receive my weekly burdens. This is not the way any of us would choose to begin our day. He does not judge nor do I ever feel judged. He is one of the most selfless and giving person I have ever met. This is easy to say because I know he is just a man. His obedience to God sets him apart. He taught me to live by grace, be long suffering, and love my wife regardless of my excuses. **(Medical Worker, Physical therapist assistant)**

Through a lifestyle of disciple making, Denny Bates has shown me what it truly means to live out Matthew 28: 19, 20. **(Educator)**

I've heard it said that on this side of eternity that there are only two things that you can be certain of: death and taxes. I'm certain of three things; the first two and that I have a friend in Denny Bates! I asked God at the beginning of my ministry to bring solid men into my life that would disciple me, teach me and hold me accountable. Denny has been an extreme answer to that prayer. **(Church-planting Pastor)**

QUALITY LEADERSHIP CONSULTANTS:
PERSONAL CONSULTING, COACHING AND COUNSELING

Our Mission: To present Quality *Ideas* that will produce Quality *Changes* in Quality *Leaders* and *Organizations*

For more information on how you and/or your organization can open the door to having a life coach join your team, please contact me. Together, lets explore the possibilities!

http://www.dennybates.com/Home/Contact.html
or via email at dennybates@gmail.com
http://www.qualityleadershipconsultants.com/
http://qualityleadershipconsultants.blogspot.com/

And on Facebook, join the Quality Leadership Consultants page

What Others Are Saying About A One Year Journey With The Shepherd:

"Denny hit a home run in Psalms of Discipleship, his sincerity in writing brings you into an atmosphere of worship and learning." Jeff Hoffart. Upper Level Manager, Business Consultant

"This wonderfully clear and doctrinally sound study is a practical tool and guide written in simple terms for everyday living. It serves to edify and inspire sincere disciples to a more intimate and worshipful relationship with our Creator. By the grace of God, Psalms of Discipleship: A One Year Journey With The Shepherd will draw disciples, with an earnest desire to develop a deeper understanding of God's Word nearer to the heart of God to live with a deeper personal relationship built upon trust and confidence in the One whose Word 'stands forever.'" Dale Locklair. B.S.; MBA; Vice President for Procurement and Construction at McLeod Health

"I am consumed with excitement and a fresh love for the Lord after reading A One Year Journey With The Shepherd!!! . . . The personal application sections are thought provoking, and attainable. I believe they are challenging in a way that creates a desire, instead of being out of reach for the growing believer." Ericka Miller, MA Clinical Counseling

"This is a great resource for anyone looking to go deeper in his or her understanding of what it means to be a disciple of Christ and what it takes to really grow in your relationship with Christ. Denny has done a great job of laying this study out in an easy to follow weekly guide on discipleship. I highly recommend this to any pastor or church leader looking for a study guide on the topic of discipleship." Lamar Younginer, B.S., M.S. College Administrator

www.ingramcontent.com/pod-product-compliance
Lightning Source LLC
Chambersburg PA
CBHW062046090426
42740CB00016B/3034